LETTERS
TO A
LEADER

LETTERS TO A LEADER

Twelve Lessons in **Being** a Leader

BILL CRITCHLEY

First published in 2021 by Libri Publishing

ISBN: 978-1-911450-74-0

A CIP catalogue record for this book is available from The British Library

Cover and book design by Carnegie Book Production

Printed in the UK by Severn

Libri Publishing
Brunel House
Volunteer Way
Faringdon
Oxfordshire
SN7 7YR

Tel: +44 (0)845 873 3837

www.libripublishing.co.uk

TESTIMONIALS FOR
LETTERS TO A LEADER

Through five powerful questions and twelve lessons in leadership,
Bill Critchley challenges prevailing assumptions on leadership whilst
provoking the reader to enquire into their own experiences of working
in and leading organisations. This book is a concise and brilliant
exploration of the key facets of leadership and combines practical
case studies with prompts for action. It is essential reading for anyone
looking to make a meaningful difference through their leadership.

Chris Askew OBE
Chief Executive, Diabetes UK

Bill has known for thirty years that, contrary to what many
business books say, real organisational life is 'messy'. (E.g. Critchley's
Law: 'the number of unintended consequences will at least equal the
number of intended consequences'.) Thankfully he also gives us a
wealth of practical lessons and tips to navigate through it in a whole
new, unexpected, practical, and deeply humane way. I can see myself
giving a copy of this book to every person I coach, and drawing
practical ideas and reassurance from my own copy for years to come.

Catherine Devitt
Chief Executive of Meyler Campbell,
a leading coach training organisation

Bill Critchley's *Letters to a Leader* brings a fresh approach to
leadership studies. Spirited and concise, the book proposes that
extra-ordinary management is best achieved when leaders are
willing to move away from conventional ideas of leadership and,
instead, are prepared to adopt a *relational* view which understands
and works within a perspective of organisations as complex,
interactive, social processes. The implications of this shift from fixed
entity to fluid process for leaders is explored via a sequence of five
'letters' packed full of practical wisdom, pertinent case vignettes, and
multiple challenges to dominant assumptions about leadership. I feel
certain that every reader of this fine book will be enriched by it.

Professor Ernesto Spinelli
Existential therapist and executive coach

ACKNOWLEDGEMENTS

I would like to acknowledge my colleague Dr Hartmut Stuelten of The Leadership Practice in Frankfurt, because he really sowed the germ of the idea for writing in the form of a 'letter to a manager', when some while ago we did some writing together, informed by our shared perspective on organisations as 'complex social processes'. For a variety of reasons, he was not able to continue, but he gave me permission to use and adapt the idea if I chose to.

I would also like to acknowledge the work of Professor Ralph Stacey, who, when he was Director of the Complexity and Management Centre at the University of Hertfordshire, inspired me with his rigorous research and thinking in adapting some of the ideas from the complexity sciences, and developing them into the perspective on organisations he described as 'complex social processes'.

Dr Patricia Shaw was an Associate Director of the Centre, and with her I had some exciting and rewarding experiences of working with this perspective in a number of assignments, some of which I draw on as vignettes in this book.

Finally, my supervisor, Professor Ernesto Spinelli was tireless in his support and encouragement, and he was willing to read and comment on a number of drafts which has made a significant difference to my developing and 'crafting' this book.

CONTENTS

INTRODUCTION

WHO SHOULD READ THIS BOOK

According to one estimate there are about 15,000 books on leadership, so why write another? The simple answer is that I think I have got something to say to the many men and women who find themselves in leadership roles, not necessarily at the top of their organisation, where a lot of the attention tends to go, but nevertheless responsible for orchestrating and co-ordinating the work of people. There have been many 'cook books' on leadership, academic treatises, case studies of successful leaders, and so forth, but I want to tell leaders what most treatises on leadership don't tell them; that there are no easy recipes or models which actually work. I want to say something about the messiness and unpredictability of being in charge but not actually in control. One of my colleagues read a draft of this short book and said everyone who is about to become a manager should be told to read it; he liked it obviously.

I recently read a book called *Seven Brief lessons on Physics* by Carlo Rovelli (Rovelli, 2014), which gave me an idea for the format of this book. I knew very little about physics, but the book was short, accessible, and seemed to distil the essence of the subject in a way which was profound yet simple. What I want to offer is exactly that, some foundational principles and lessons which are simple and accessible and 'right minded'.

What I mean by 'right minded' is that, when you read them, I would hope that they will resonate with your experience of the messy reality of life as you find it. They will not always be 'obvious' because I shall be bringing some thinking and ideas about organisations and psychology which run counter to some conventional perspectives, but they will be practical and grounded in my own long experience as a Business Director of Ashridge Consulting, an organisational psychologist, a change facilitator, a leadership coach and a psychotherapist.

Most of us will have some immediate associations with the notion of leadership, either from our experience of what is lacking (and there is much talk of that as I write this book in the UK during the Covid pandemic) or from our experience of being led, attempting to lead, or from ideas about leadership which we have read or appear to have been exemplified by known figures. I am not intending to reprise the conventional ways of describing 'styles' of leadership (e.g. autocratic, bureaucratic, democratic and so on), but I do want to start by addressing what seem to me to be two particularly popular ways of thinking about leadership, the first being what has become something of a leadership 'myth', and the second being its association with power.

MYTHS OF LEADERSHIP

LEADER AS HERO

Firstly, there is a largely mythic view of leader as hero, which is upheld in our collective imagination by stories of some iconic figures, such as Gandhi, Mandela, Lincoln, Washington, Roosevelt, Churchill, to name a few. In some ways these mythical figures, or exemplars of leadership, are not particularly helpful to the many people who find themselves in 'ordinary' leadership roles in business, public and third-sector organisations. They have acquired a heroic status in our imagination, which does not mean to say that they were not heroic or remarkable people in some ways, but it is not helpful or sensible to hold them up as models of leadership to be emulated in today's organisations. Heroic leadership does not work particularly well in organisations where the trend has been to a more distributed or 'empowering' form of leadership. Also, these were all political leaders.

Political leaders are often motivated by power for its own sake, or by the perceived need to win power, or to keep a particular party in power, or by some ideology, whereas a leader of an organisation's primary task is to mobilise the organisation to be effective in achieving its purpose. I have often consulted to the UK Civil Service, and to various types of local authorities, where there is a tension between the politicians' agenda to follow a particular party line, and the officers' agenda to deliver effective services for their community. Hence I want to make this distinction between organisational and political leadership, because this book is primarily intended for those who have leadership roles in organisations.

POWER; FORMAL AND INFORMAL AUTHORITY

Secondly, leadership is popularly associated with authority, and there is no question that most senior leaders have some degree of formal authority bestowed on them. This is vested in their position in the hierarchy, from which they can prescribe what they want to be done; they also have the power to affect someone's career by recommending them, promoting them and, ultimately, they can get people fired or made redundant. They wield sanctions which affect people's livelihood, their sense of security and often their sense of self-worth.

The possibility of such sanctions often evokes among their followers some degree of compliance or even fear, which is rarely a helpful motivation, and in my experience many leaders over-rely on their formal authority. You may prescribe as much as you like, but if you make unreasonable demands, or have unrealistic expectations, you will be ineffective over the longer term. If you fail to bring people with you, to enable them to find their own motivation or purpose, the part of the organisation for which you are responsible will not flourish.

So, while it is important to acknowledge that you are likely to have some 'formal' authority, if you do not learn how to engage and mobilise your people, you will not be effective as a manager or leader. This book is largely devoted to suggesting how you might develop your informal authority or 'soft power' as it is sometimes known, alongside your formal authority.

Some people take up a 'leading' role by taking initiatives to get things done, with no formal authority. As a matter of fact, everyone is capable of developing soft power, and in that sense, you are no different from anyone else, except that you have a designated role which carries with it some formal authority. It could be said that everyone is capable of leading, through taking initiatives or finding solutions to problems which lie outside their defined area of responsibility – taking a lead in meetings by contributing ideas and views and so forth – but many people do not step up to this challenge. This may be because they are afraid of displeasing you, their boss, or of speaking out against the received wisdom, and this might be the consequence of your over-relying on your formal power. By so doing you will inhibit people and lose their intelligence and contribution, whereas your main job is actually to mobilise their intelligence and contribution. This is what is meant by 'empowering' people, but 'empowerment' in my experience, is often more honoured in the breach than the observance.

As a consultant I am an informal leader too; I have no formal authority except that I may 'borrow' authority from my client if he or she is a senior leader. Otherwise I have to rely on my ability to engage and influence, to propose and respond to what emerges, so I shall be drawing on my own experience as an informal leader as well as my observations, reflections and theorising.

The book takes the form of five 'letters', each starting with a question, followed by a 'principle', and a number of 'lessons' which can be inferred from each principle. Although these principles are really interdependent and mutually supporting, I think some linear structure is useful in moving from theory to practice. I want this book to be practical, because I think if more leaders were to adopt these 'lessons', organisations would be more sustainable places in which to live, as well as being more effective. They have not, as far as I know, been widely written about, and come from my own personal experience over the years I have worked as a leader and an organisation psychologist, having coached many leaders and their teams, designed and led leadership development assignments, and facilitated many change initiatives.

FIVE CORE QUESTIONS

Each of the five letters starts by posing a question. These questions are provocations to your practice as a leader, and each one gives rise to a 'theory', or perspective in the form of what I have called a principle. These are the questions I shall be inviting you to consider:

1. How do you think about this thing we call an 'organisation'? Have you thought about it at all? If you start to think about it you may find it rather elusive. Back in the 1990s, Gareth Morgan (Morgan, 1997) pondered this question and came to the view that the phenomenon we experience, which we call 'organisation', has no material reality, and we can only attempt to describe it through metaphor. These metaphors tend to be unconscious, but, as Morgan says, whatever metaphor informs you will lead you to focus on some aspects of organisation and ignore others. *Letter one* invites you to reflect on your informing assumptions and suggests that there is a way of thinking about the 'reality' of organisations which does not rely on metaphor and which makes more sense of your lived experience.

2. Have you been conditioned to think that when push comes to shove, the buck stops with you? Paradoxically this is probably true, but do you make decisions on your own and announce them to your colleagues, or do you routinely involve others in your decision-making, and if so, how do you go about this? *Letter two* suggests that the practice of 'inclusive' leadership requires a leader to enable and orchestrate rather than command and control, which puts a premium on how you show up as a person. As Reed Hastings of Netflix put it, *'to be a better leader you have to be a better person'.*

3. How much have you thought about the quality of your communication? You have probably heard a lot about the importance of good communication, but apart from possibly thinking about going on a course to develop your presentation skills, you may not have considered the possibility that 'communicating' is all you really do as a leader,

that 'communication' is your main currency. In *Letter three* I propose that there are two main kinds of communication, and while the most obvious kind tends to be associated with the 'formal' aspects of a leader's role, the more complex and subtle kind is associated with the *informal* aspects of your role, which constitutes most of what you do.

4. What is your relationship with your own team, and how well does it work, *as a team?* It is something of a truism to say that choosing and developing your team is one of the most important tasks you have. Unfortunately, team working in modern, functionally designed organisations, does not come easily, particularly as most western organisations are predicated on an engineering assumption about the importance of each part performing effectively. *Letter four* explores what it takes to create a real team out of a group of functionally orientated managers, and offers you some tried and tested ways of developing your team.

5. What is your purpose? Do you have a personal purpose, or do you take it for granted that it is your job to fulfil the organisation's purpose? If you do have a sense of personal purpose, do you see it in purely financial terms or does it extend beyond financial goals? *Letter five* explores this somewhat vexed question of personal purpose, and challenges you to think about what kind of difference you really want to make in your role as a leader. It also suggests how you move from the *what* (purpose), to the *how* (strategy).

I do not want this to be a conventional academic book, backed by conventional research and full of references; I see no point in parroting what other people have said or written, and I am confident I would say little new. However, I have been informed by particular writers and perspectives which make sense to me, and where appropriate, I shall of course acknowledge and reference them.

METHODOLOGY

The question you might ask is how have I derived these principles? Have I plucked them out of the air? What research have I done? They have largely been derived from my experience, as I said above, as a Business Director of Ashridge Consulting, an organisational psychologist, a change facilitator, a leadership developer, a coach, and a psychotherapist, and, also, from my time running a Masters and Doctoral programme at Ashridge Business School. This academic extension of my role required me to turn my experience into some kind of research-based 'evidence'. The methodology I learnt and developed over time is a form of 'action research', in which I am adopting an 'attitude of inquiry'; I observe, question, reflect, read, draw some tentative conclusions, and experiment in my work, cycling iteratively, continuously and somewhat messily through this lifelong process.

Through my work with leaders I observe what they actually do; I inquire into what was going on for them when they made certain decisions or took particular actions; I am interested in whether they consulted anyone, whether they were reacting to events, or some inner drive to be active, to control, to pressure from a boss or other stakeholders; how thoughtful they were, and what was their 'theory in use', and so on. Chris Argyris (Argyris, 1977) makes a very useful distinction between 'espoused' theory, and 'theory in use', and while most organisations have plenty of espoused theories, about diversity, integrity, respecting people and so forth, much of it verging on the banal or cliché, leaders rarely risk reflecting on their theory in use. For example, do they reflect on whether they actually tolerate and welcome difference of views (diversity) or whether they are disinclined to take account of, or even listen to, views which challenge their own? When they speak harshly to someone who has displeased them in some way, do they really care about how consistent it might be with the espoused value of respect?

More importantly I observed the impact they seemed to have on others and inquired into what they evoked in others. You might also expect me to have been interested in the effects of their actions on 'the organisation', and of course I was, in the way that I shall describe later – particularly in the intended and unintended consequences. From some thirty years of this kind of practice, I have attempted to synthesise these principles and their attendant lessons from my experience and continuing *inquiry*.

The first principle includes a fair bit of theory and, as I promised something practical, may at first glance seem overly academic, as well as being counter intuitive. I ask you to stick with it because the particular perspective on organisations on which I am about to expound, informs much of the rest of the book. For some it may seem a somewhat radical view, challenging many of the conventional nostrums which have informed management theory and discourse for decades; but that is the point of writing this book. I think many of the assumptions about the nature of organisation, and hence the nature of leadership, turn out to be flawed.

This is not just my view, by the way; I quote many who share it, some of whom have had a major influence on my own development. But it takes a while before a paradigm shifts, as Thomas Kuhn in his book *The Structure of Scientific Revolutions* (Kuhn, 1962), points out. An emerging new view on some aspect of how the world works at first seems preposterous, and advocates of this emerging view are dismissed as eccentrics, unmoored from reality, or even heretics (think of Copernicus). Gradually the new perspective is taken up by early adopters and, at some point, becomes taken for granted. I would say that the view I am about to propound has been taken up by a number of early adopters, and if you are one of these, you will not find anything I am about to suggest controversial. But it is by no means mainstream, so I am working on the assumption that, for many of you, it may be unfamiliar territory. Hence I am taking the time to elaborate on what I see as a fundamental shift which I think needs to take place in how we think about this phenomenon we call 'organisation'.

LETTER ONE:
THE PHENOMENON WE CALL 'ORGANISATION'

Dear Leader

How do you think about this thing we call an 'organisation'? Have you thought about it at all? If you start to think about it you may find it rather elusive. Back in 1997, Gareth Morgan (Morgan, 1997) pondered this question and came to the view that the phenomenon we experience called 'organisation' had no material reality and we could only attempt to describe it through metaphor. Morgan's book *Images of Organisation* is a useful one to have on your bookshelf, because he was one of the first writers to challenge, in a very accessible way, some of the taken-for-granted assumptions we make about organisations.

I agree with him that an organisation is not a 'thing' with a material essence, and that metaphors do indeed tend to be how we think about them and describe them, but as he points out, there are many different metaphors in play and the one which informs you, will also inform how you lead, so it needs thinking about.

My own view, which has been particularly informed by the work of Ralph Stacey and his colleagues at the University of Hertfordshire (Stacey et al., 2000), with whom I was associated over a long period of time, is that there is a way of thinking about the 'reality' of organisations which does not rely on metaphor, and this is what I want to elaborate in principle one. For those of you who are interested in exploring in more depth the theories informing the principle I am about to introduce, the book *Complexity and Management: Fad or Radical Challenge to Systems Thinking?* (ibid), by Stacey et al. is well worth getting hold of, but it is a book for those of you who like wrestling with theory.

PRINCIPLE ONE: 'ORGANISATIONS' ARE COMPLEX SOCIAL PROCESSES

As I said, I think we need to make more explicit how we think about the concept of 'organisation' because the way leaders think about organisations, their assumptions and underlying frame of reference will determine how they think and act as leaders.

The perspective I intend to offer challenges the largely engineering view of organisations which still prevails (one of Morgan's metaphors) and suggests that organisations are 'complex social processes'. Although I am writing about it as one principle there are a number of important implications which flow from it, and I shall highlight these in italics.

Conventional management thinking tends to treat organisations as if they were objects in nature with properties which can be ascertained through diligent analysis, in the same way that scientific exploration proceeds, and this way of thinking also tends to treat them as if they are machines to be engineered. If we listen to the discourse in most organisations we will hear such words as 'engineering', 'driving', 'leveraging' rather frequently; such words betoken an engineering mindset.

An alternative way of thinking, and one that is, in my view, closer to our lived experience – and supported by the emerging study of complexity – is to think of organisations as complex social processes. They are social in the sense that they consist of people in an ongoing process of interaction, deciding together what to do and how to do it; and they are complex in the sense that interactions are non-linear, meaning that effects can rarely be traced back to any single cause, as this process of interaction is continuous and simultaneous. The noun 'organisation' cannot capture what is in effect an ongoing 'process of communicative interaction'.

The sociologist George Herbert Mead (Mead, 1967) described this process of communicative interaction rather succinctly by saying that 'the meaning of a gesture is in the response' (Mead 1967, p. 146).

He used the word 'gesture' to mean any communicative move, verbal or physical, towards another. While as humans we gesture with intention – for example I want to convey some information to you, ask you to do something, scare you, convince you or whatever – it is only in your response that the 'meaning' of the interaction emerges. If you think about it, this means you can never know how someone is going to respond to your communicative gesture, and if you think about it a bit more, you will realise that in an organisation of say, one thousand people, with everyone 'gesturing' to each other all the time, how unpredictable and uncontrollable an organisation really is.

The interactions that we have with each other simply create more interactions. Our interactions do not add up to a whole, a construct beloved of many OD practitioners, because they continuously evolve. Neither is any stable or bigger thing behind peoples' interactions. There is not 'the company' that does something to people, there are only individual people relating to each other. Managers may perceive themselves as standing 'objectively', outside the system in order to work on it, but this is an illusion; there is no 'thing' to be outside, as we are all participants, forming and being formed by a continuous *process of communicative interaction.*

JOINT ACTION

Of course, there are some relatively stable patterns of interaction which enable the everyday operational tasks to be routinely achieved. These are sustained through designed, legitimate networks of roles and accountabilities through which people pursue official goals and policies, and intentions, as articulated by senior managers. These intentions are usually expressed through purpose or mission statements, strategies, financial plans and all of that, and these are extremely important in providing guidelines for action, and 'orchestrating' and co-ordinating 'joint action'. When done well, they can also contribute to providing people with a sense of purpose and identity, and by 'doing it well' I mean engaging people more widely in the process of developing plans and strategy, as opposed to the Board sitting in a room with a hot towel around their collective heads and then emerging to pronounce the outcome of their deliberations to an audience waiting in breathless anticipation. I say more about this in letter five.

Many textbooks on how to achieve effectiveness and efficiency – usually seen as a *sine qua non* of achieving financial objectives – focus on designing and improving these 'formal' processes and procedures, stressing the importance of 'alignment' and 'consistency'. Consistency and repeatability are necessary for many production and operational procedures, but the paradox is that while stable routines which produce consistency are necessary, they can also be inimical to innovation.

INNOVATION

Fortunately, at the same time as managers strive to create formal processes and procedures, the operation of many *informal networks* in which significant political, social and other processes are at work, gives rise to a degree of unpredictability, often bemoaned by managers. But therein lies the potential for innovation which arises through the *interaction of difference*. This is rather an important point because the emphasis on alignment and consistency to achieve quality improvement, whilst being important and necessary, also inhibits innovation. 'If you always do what you've always done, you always get what you've always got' (anon). Innovation arises in the ongoing messy iteration of different views, the inevitable conflict which occurs in all political processes, where people compete for attention and resources driven by the desire to further their own priorities and visions.

Many treatises have been written about how to achieve innovation, but they tend to be informed by the same thinking which creates alignment, and are informed by the same belief in planning and control. Therefore, what they usually offer is some kind of plannable process to achieve innovation. I know some organisations who have appointed a Director of Change as if it were a function to be led. With a mindset of planning and control it is hard to embrace the idea that innovation arises from the interaction of difference, or to put it simply, messiness.

This is highly paradoxical for leaders because they need to create and develop processes and procedures to manage the core business of today, while at the same time, being 'disrupters' to ensure that the organisation continuously innovates and renews itself. This is a real challenge. I remember coming across one competence in a competency framework for global leaders, which was labelled 'cognitive complexity'. I think this rather aptly sums up the personal challenge for many leaders schooled in the importance of being in control.

The diagram below attempts to depict the leader's paradox. In this diagram I have described what is needed to manage the core business of today as 'ordinary management', and what is needed to create the context of innovation as 'extraordinary management'. I am using the terms 'ordinary' and 'extraordinary' literally, and don't intend to suggest that 'extraordinary' is better than 'ordinary', merely that leaders have two rather different and apparently incompatible roles to fulfil, often at the same time, because innovation is needed to continuously challenge and refresh the normal and regular ways we 'do things round here', as well as create novelty.

When you come to the second diagram I use in this book to talk about team development, you will notice many similarities. I know that the second diagram was developed my me and my colleague at the time, David Casey, and I *think* that Ralph Stacey produced a similar matrix later, which I have adapted considerably, but I can't find it anywhere to reference it. As I said about linear causality, it is hard sometimes to trace what comes from where!

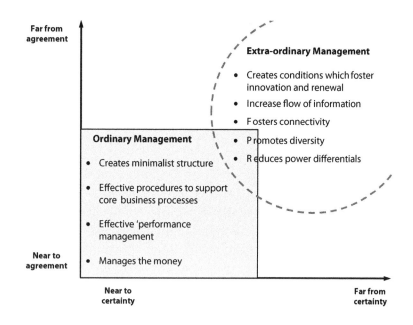

Professor Bill Critchley

There are many famous examples of new products and services which have come about as unintended consequences of some other activity, for example the famous story of Post-it notes. In 1968, Dr Spencer Silver, a scientist at 3M in the United States, was attempting to develop a super-strong adhesive. Instead, he accidentally created a 'low-tack', reusable, pressure-sensitive adhesive. Arthur Fry is then credited with utilising 3M's officially sanctioned 'permitted bootlegging' policy to develop the idea.

Seeing organisations as 'social processes' provides a different perspective on how change and innovation really occur, and suggests that *creating the conditions for innovation*, as shown in the dotted half-circle above, (for example by legitimising disagreement, encouraging and supporting initiatives, reducing power differentials, cherishing anomalies, nourishing 'out of the box' thinking and so forth), works better than creating roles to lead change, or trying to set up formal processes to generate innovation.

'PATTERNS EMERGE WITHOUT A MASTER PLAN'

People lower down an organisation's hierarchy often assume that there is a grand master plan which directs and controls everything. The inconvenient truth is that there is no grand master plan, only intentions, and while these intentions serve an important purpose, as described above, everyone knows that none of these plans and strategies are ever achieved as written. Many years ago, the Royal Dutch Shell oil company realised that its strategic planning process was over elaborate, took up too much resource and was of little value. They saw it as flawed in its attempt to predict future market demand, determine their desired strategic position and extrapolate backwards to create a plan. I think nowadays it has become much more obvious that as global and market context changes continuously, there is no way any linear plan, predicated on some assumptions about, and desires for the future, could be achieved as written. I write more about this in lesson nine on strategy. To take account of this inherent unpredictability, Shell developed what they called 'scenario planning', whereby they worked up a number of future scenarios to better inform how they might respond and adapt to differing scenarios; one might see it as an exercise in developing agility and innovative capability.

Although organisations cannot, in the long run, be predicted or controlled, through the multitude of local interactions overall *patterns* emerge. In other words, although no one is in overall control of the totality of people's local interactions, some kind of *order* does emerge, although it cannot be predicted. Complex responsive process theory calls this phenomenon *self-organisation*, and Stuart Kauffman, an American medical doctor, theoretical biologist, and complex systems researcher, had one of those 'aha!' moments, when he discovered that 'self-organisation' is a fundamental property of natural systems. As he put it, in his book *At Home in the Universe* (Kauffman, 1996), roughly paraphrased, 'order emerges for free; you don't have to make it happen'.

If we translate this principle to social processes, it implies that order emerges without leaders having to make it happen, at least without having to try quite so hard to be 'in control'. Everyone in an organisation works within some frameworks of intent, some overall 'rules'. As a leader you do not need to worry that if you were to give your subordinates some directions as to what you saw as the strategic priorities, and left them to find their own way of achieving them, some kind of anarchy would occur. Quite the reverse; what would be most likely to happen is that they would find their own way to achieve your priorities, but being closer to the issues than you, it might be a much more creative and effective way than if you had issued detailed instructions.

'BEING IN CHARGE BUT NOT IN CONTROL' – THE SYSTEMIC NATURE OF ORGANISATIONS

'Being in charge but not in control' was the title of a fellow student's PhD thesis at Hertfordshire University. He came to realise that, while he was paid as a supply chain manager to be 'in charge', he could never be 'in control', another inconvenient truth for those who advocate a version of management which is predicated on the importance of gaining control.

Organisations are *systemic* in nature. Systemic is another concept often used to characterise the patterns of interaction and connection which I have described above, and it is a useful shorthand to remind us of the interconnected nature of organisational process in which a movement in one part may well, like the proverbial butterfly flapping its wings and causing a typhoon, amplify or change an organisational pattern – but equally, it may not. Change occurs when some small deviation in a pattern becomes amplified.

As an example, some years ago, I was sitting in our normal monthly management meeting, with my usual colleagues, in the usual setting, at the usual time. One of my colleagues raised what she saw as a problem we had as a leadership team, namely that people in the organisation saw us as lacking transparency, did not know what we discussed or what decisions we were making. Our boss attempted to dampen her concern by saying that all employees in most organisations said the same kind of thing about the leadership team. If this had followed the normal course of events, the issue would have gone away and we would have continued to wade through the normal agenda items.

On this occasion however, someone else chipped in and said, 'Actually I agree with that and I do think we have a serious credibility problem', and then others agreed. The boss finally conceded that maybe we did have a problem and we came up with what we thought was a rather radical experiment; we all agreed to hold our meetings in open session, and invite people to attend if they wanted to. The difference which emerged was thus amplified and the pattern shifted to a different kind of meeting in a different space and potentially, a different configuration. This is how I think change happens, not through careful planning but often quite spontaneously. Our boss could have used her power to dampen the emerging change, but did not do so, and so a small difference was amplified into a significant pattern change.

I argue later that grasping the 'systemic' nature of all social processes is essential to understand why things so rarely turn out as planned, and it will help you to better *anticipate* the number of potential consequences of taking a particular course of action and realise the futility of over-elaborate planning systems.

Managers have to act with intention, on the expectation of a desirable outcome, at the same time knowing that a specific outcome will not materialise exactly as intended, requiring them to be ready for whatever the outcome will be. This simultaneous knowing of one's intention while not knowing the consequences of one's action, generates much, usually undisclosed, anxiety, given that most managers and consultants are expected to deliver specific, pre-determined outcomes. This presents one of the most fundamental challenges for managers living within a deterministic paradigm where the assumption of linear dynamics of cause and effect still predominates. Coming to understand the non-linear dynamics of complex processes could have a liberating and normalising effect on management practice.

LESSON ONE: CONTEXT IS ALL

You can infer from principle one, namely that an organisation is a complex social process which is systemic in nature, that no organisational context is the same, so the kind of leadership that is called for in one context is unlikely to be applicable to another. While I think there are some transferable foundational skills, some of which I am offering as 'lessons', leadership is not generally a transportable body of knowledge and capability, but is highly context dependent.

The conventional view of leadership tends to be preoccupied with the leader as an individual. This view assumes the leader to be capable of detachment and objectivity in relation to what is being led. The focus tends to be on clarifying the leader's roles (e.g. strategist, planner, decision-maker, motivator etc) and on analysing the situation prior to taking individual action. I would categorise this as an instrumental perspective on organisations which gives rise to a transactional model of leadership.

The development logic, which follows from this set of assumptions, would be to analyse required competences, develop skills, and provide tools and techniques. If that really made sense in the light of my experience, I would not bother to write this book as we already have legions of competency frameworks.

While I think there are these foundational skills or 'lessons' which I am developing in this book, a leader is embedded in, and shaped by a particular context, part of which is made up of the norms, rituals, values, and patterns of interaction and behaviour which have emerged over time. These both constrain and enable leaders; for example, if you are a partner in a law firm, it is much more difficult to manage the performance of a fellow partner working on your assignment than it would be in a more hierarchical corporate company. On the other hand, you would probably have more freedom to work in your own way.

THE TIP OF THE ICEBERG

I failed to take account of the importance of context when I worked with a UK retailer's leadership team, where the MD was aware that he tended to dominate the team's major decision-making, while the team tended to retreat to their functional and departmental responsibilities. He sensed that the team needed to develop their capability to work as a collective decision-making body (see lesson nine).

We did some very good work during workshops ('away-days') to shift their way of working to a more 'dialogic' form, and become less reliant on PowerPoint presentations, often brought to the meeting by one of their subordinates. After one such away-day I felt so encouraged that I wrote them all an email, appreciating the progress they had made and suggesting that our work was done.

As part of my engagement I had also been asked to attend their regular meetings to help them consolidate their learning from the 'away-days'. I arrived at the last one I was to attend, which was a two-day, half-yearly strategic review, with high expectations, but was dismayed to see them default to their old patterns, with subordinates turning up to make PowerPoint presentations (their day in the sun!), and the usual desultory picking at points in the presentations, and the Managing Director, as usual summing up and proposing next steps.

On reflection, both on my own and with the team, I realised I had only been dealing with the 'tip of the iceberg'. This team was embedded in long-established norms and patterns of behaviour; if they were to change their way of working, they had to ask for radically different kinds of involvement from subordinates, often involving their not attending meetings, or inviting them to participate rather than present, and much more besides.

This example highlights the extent to which leaders are embedded in context, and hence, to a large extent, always shaped by it. It is one thing to work differently in a half-day development workshop, with a facilitator guiding the process, and quite another when a team is once again embedded in their normal context.

The major implication of recognising your contextual dependence is that you focus less on the capability and performance of individuals and pay more attention to the pattern of interactions which give rise to particular behaviours in which you participate.

A VIEW FROM A SEASONED PROFESSIONAL

Marvin Weisborg, one of those American organisation development consultants who were influential in shaping the practice of 'OD', was working at Ashridge Business School (in his eighties – there's hope for us all!), when they were embarking on a fairly major change process. He sent me this reply to my question about what he focused on in his work:

'I came to organisation development and I immersed myself in applied behavioural science. It took me some years, and working with some experienced colleagues, to realise that structure is a powerful influence on behaviour. I did not know that when I embarked on training in behavioural science. Since then, I have not sought to change people, only the *conditions under which they interact.* Working that way, I freed myself from a lot of attempts to change individual behaviour which still preoccupies some practitioners'.

In summary I am proposing a move away from the conventional transactional view of leadership, in which you conceive yourself as a rational actor, informed by your perceived understanding of cause and effect, taking objective action in order to produce a predictable effect (what you think you are supposed to do), to a *relational perspective.* With this perspective, you, as the leader, acknowledge that you are also a participant in a systemic context, shaping and being shaped by it, albeit with some formal authority as described above, and with some ability to *anticipate* possible outcomes, but with little ability to predict any particular outcome. Leaders and managers realise this intuitively, but think they are supposed to know what they are doing and to be able to predict outcomes for their bosses and shareholders. The fact that they can't do what they think they are supposed to be able to do can be very stressful.

It helps to understand the Critchley law of unintended consequences which suggests, somewhat unscientifically, that the number of unintended consequences will be at least equal to the number of intended consequences. This could be quite liberating if only your bosses and shareholders also understood this. My good friend Patricia Shaw once said that 'strategy is the interaction between chance and intention'. I don't know whether it was original to her, but it seems nicely aphoristic and wise.

LESSON TWO: IT'S WHAT YOU DO NEXT THAT MATTERS

As the first principle suggests, members of an organisation are all participants in creating a social process which continuously evolves into an unknown future. We cannot, by definition, get outside it; as participants we simultaneously create and are created by the process of engaging together in joint action.

In the same way that the future is unknowable, the past is also unknowable in the sense that everyone will have their own story about 'what happened', and because this process of interaction is non-linear, which means that there are always a multiplicity of actions occurring and interacting simultaneously, there can rarely be one cause of anything, but always a multiplicity of causes interacting together. In other words, there is no point wasting your time looking for who is to blame.

Too much enquiry into the so-called 'root' of a problem is a waste of time because there is unlikely to be one root cause. This proposition may sound counter intuitive if you have been schooled to analyse problems, identify causes and to find solutions. Such an approach rests on two false assumptions, which you can infer from what I have already said, one being that the circumstances which gave rise to 'the problem' will be repeated in exactly the same way, and the other being the assumption of linear cause and effect relationships. As I suggested earlier, organisations are non-linear and complex, so the probability that the exact same circumstances will recur is close to zero.

It follows from this that your attention should be on what is happening, or being enacted now, in the 'living present', rather than what happened in the past, which cannot be changed and is unlikely to recur in exactly the same way. Of course, the past, as well as our future anticipations, shape the present, but I am suggesting the smart money will be on what you are going to do next, rather than launching an enquiry into the past, which the smart money will see as deflection or 'wheel spinning'.

I was recently asked to work with the leadership group of a public sector organisation on the subject of leadership behaviour. This had been largely provoked by a people survey in which the scores on 'bullying, harassment and discrimination' were very concerning. Leaders tended to refer to it as 'the BHD score', and in my view, reducing these rather concerning behaviours to an acronym served as a way of not really having to hear and acknowledge how some leaders appeared to be behaving.

I took the view that these scores were evidence of some behavioural patterns, but I thought it would be important not to obsess about the scores; knowing the kind of people these were, I anticipated they might find it easier to try and understand the 'data' and where it came from rather than accept there were some systemic behavioural dynamics for which, as the leaders in the organisation, they were jointly responsible.

I talked to many people in the organisation and discovered that some preferred to describe these behaviours as 'robust' or 'emphatic', or in some way inevitable. Most people, however, had experienced or witnessed a degree of shouting, swearing and, in some cases, bullying, which was seen by the majority as unacceptable and not congruent with their aspiration to be inspiring, confident, empowering and 'inclusive'.

I convened a half day's meeting of the leadership group, which I opened by saying; 'I want to give you the freedom to talk about this pattern of behaviour among yourselves, to have a dialogue, which I will prompt with a number of questions, the first of which is, 'To what extent you see this as an issue? How important is it'? My next two questions were, 'What are your intentions in behaving in this way, and how have they become instituted?'

Later I offered a final observation and question, 'This behaviour really stands out in relation to most organisations I have worked with or am aware of, and I wonder what it is about this organisation that generates such an extreme version?'

This 'dialogue' was welcomed by almost everyone, and the CEO stood up quite early on and said that he was part of the problem, which was extremely useful. I came away feeling rather pleased with how I had set it up, and proposed a second session configured around this question, 'Let's assume that everyone around this table is part of this behavioural pattern, or at least colludes with it in some way, do you intend to change it, and if so, what will be needed, from you as a leadership group, and as individuals?'

At this next session I tried to put them into groups to talk about what they intended to do next, but they kept resisting my suggestion, saying that they wanted to continue the dialogue in the large group. It seemed they were comfortable talking *about* the problem and how it came about and were really unwilling or unable to grasp the nettle of *what to do next*.

LESSON THREE:
BEST PRACTICE IS AN ILLUSION

Because you are embedded in a specific context, and hence always shaped by context, leadership is 'called forth' by a particular context and cannot be seen independently from it. It follows from this that it is not a good use of your time looking out there for 'best practice'; you might learn something interesting from what other organisations do, but it is always a mistake to import some methodology or technology wholesale into your organisation.

For example, Agile Management thinking is being applied by many organisations with the key principles tending to be described as the law of the small team, the law of the customer, and the law of the network. When I look at what is meant by these principles, they look fairly congruent with the principles I am advocating, and in the same way they can be adapted to your particular context in going about a change initiative.

However, Agile is also know for a number of techniques like the scrum methodology, Kanban, and so forth. In my experience, these tend to be imported and applied wholesale without much regard for context, and fail to produce the desired outcome. Tools, models and techniques can be useful aids to stimulate new forms of conversation, but you can't turn the handle of a model and expect a useful answer to come out, so don't over-rely on them.

IDEAS FOR ACTION

- Do not waste too much time and energy on finding what went wrong (the 'why')
- Instead ask the questions, preferably with others, what have we learnt; what went well, and what might we do differently?
- Decide, preferably with others, on the next moves (the 'what'); *plan, do, review* is a simple but useful 'action inquiry' cycle.

- From time to time, and particularly if your attempts to solve a specific problem seem to be ineffective, ask yourself:
  - o What does the context (patterns or dynamics) evoke in you; how are you feeling, in particular how are you tending to react (see lesson 5)?
  - o What are **you** doing to sustain the pattern?
  - o What might be a different response that might challenge or interrupt the *pattern*? Here are some further thoughts about the nature of repetitive or 'stuck' patterns:

In a book called *Change: Principles of Problem Formulation and Resolution*, Watzlawick, Wheatland and Fisch (Watzlawick, 1974) identified some archetypal patterns of stuckness. They defined 'Stuckness' as repeated attempts to solve a problem which only succeeded in reinforcing the problem. They described four archetypical patterns of 'Stuckness': 'trying harder', 'if only' solutions, 'Utopian' solutions and 'setting paradoxes'.

'Trying harder' speaks for itself; 'if only' solutions are when we conveniently locate the problems somewhere else, rather than acknowledging our part in the problem, e.g. if only we had a properly functioning CRM system. 'Utopian' solutions describes an idealised 'all singing, all dancing' total solution which takes little account of things as they actually are; I talk more about this later in the book.

'Setting paradoxes' is what Gregory Bateson (Bateson, 1972) described as putting people in a double bind, and one of the best examples I observed was when a Chief Executive of a client organisation exhorted people to take more initiatives; clearly if I take more initiatives because my boss requires me to, then I am not taking an initiative, and if I comply with his request, it is highly likely that the initiative will have in some way, to please the boss.

The key point the authors make is that the stuckness is created by the attempts to solve the problem, so the attempts to solve the problem **become** the problem. For example, if an organisation's revenue is insufficient to generate a required level of profit, it has a problem, but it is not stuck. If repeated attempts to increase the revenue only succeed in raising costs, reducing margin, increasing effort and not increasing profit, then it is stuck.

LETTER TWO: INCLUSIVITY

Dear Leader

Have you been conditioned to think that when push comes to shove, the buck stops with you? Paradoxically this is probably true, but do you make decisions on your own and announce them to your colleagues, or do you routinely involve others in your decision-making?

W. L. Gore and Associates are known for their non-hierarchical management model. Bill Gore, one of the founders wanted to support human fulfilment, embodied in a set of principles and management practices designed to foster trust, initiative and the emergence of natural leaders. One of their principles, roughly paraphrased, is; 'never make an important decision on your own; always ask some good people first'.

I intend to expand on this in my second principle, which I am calling 'inclusivity'.

PRINCIPLE TWO: INCLUSIVITY

Inclusivity has become a popular construct in writing about leadership; indeed, it figured in the title of a recent HBR article (Bourke, 2020) and I shall use it because it does resonate with the process principle expanded above.

The process perspective, described in principle one, asserts that an organisation is not a fixed entity or thing, but a constant process of gesturing and responding **between** people. A leader is, along with everyone else, *included* in a relational process with fellow embodied human beings, and it behoves her to communicate in a way which acknowledges the subjective and co-created nature of her communication.

FEELING INCLUDED

In my personal experience I worked for a managing director who was particularly good at 'grasping the nettle', or naming the imperative, whether it was winning more business, improving profitability or whatever. He would tend to say something along these lines: 'We have to solve this problem; I don't have the answer but I do know that if we all work together, we have the intelligence and experience to solve it'. My response to this was to feel trusted and *included*; I knew he was not going to impose his solution and that I was going to be asked, indeed required to make a serious and committed contribution. Inclusive leaders tend to use the pronoun 'we' rather than 'I'.

AN INCLUSIVE PROCESS FOR DEVELOPING STRATEGIC PRIORITIES

In another example I was working with a mental health trust where the CEO wanted to develop a clear set of 'strategic' priorities. She may not have used this word but she wanted an inclusive process, and I, with my colleagues, suggested she bring all managers, from across the whole organisation, together for two days in what we called a 'large group' conver-sation. This is quite a courageous thing for any CEO to do, as these processes can get quite messy and the leadership team can feel seriously out of control, as indeed can we, the consult-ants! As it happened, what emerged was the realisation that the rather siloed structure of the organisations was impeding the collaboration which was absolutely necessary to address their strategic priorities; a radical re-configuring of the organi-sation structure occurred during those two days, and it was her courage and willingness to go with such a radical outcome that allowed this to happen.

I could give other examples of what I am calling inclusive leadership, but I think that you will begin to realise that the practice of inclusive leadership requires a leader to enable and orchestrate rather than command and control. My own maxim is that the leader's job is to 'mobilise the collective intelligence of the organisation'.

LESSON FOUR: LEADING IS HUMAN AND RIGHT-MINDED

In my experience, many managers, on being promoted to leadership, assume they have to act like a leader. Maybe they think a leader is supposed to distance themselves from those they lead, to be slightly aloof, or distant, to look knowing or strong or decisive or even ruthless; in other words, there is a coat to be worn to disguise or cover up one's ordinary humanity.

> ### THE EMPEROR HAS NO CLOTHES
>
> In an early part of my career, I was a brand manager for Lever Bros. I noticed that people expended a lot of intellectual sweat on writing brand plans and advertising strategies; the name of the game was to write well in a particular style demanded by the marketing director, and this seemed to be the most important performance currency, so I attempted to don this mask of intellectual rigour. I then had an epiphany when I and my boss, and two even more senior people were gathered around a poster for a dishwashing detergent, four expensive 'suits' worried about whether the colour was the right yellow. From this moment I started to see through some of the pretensions of management and how removed they can get, in this case from the simple task of making and selling detergent!

Wearing some kind of coat or mask is very stressful and it certainly does not promote trust or enable inclusivity. In this fourth lesson I want to suggest that leading is founded on exactly the same qualities as those required by ordinary, everyday relating. They are, in a way, commonplace, but also tend, even in ordinary everyday interactions, to be more 'honoured in the breach than the observance'. I speak of such things as care and courtesy, a reasonable degree of empathy, of good intention. This last perhaps encapsulates best what I mean; by good intention I mean the intent not to harm, the intent to take the other's interests and context into account, the intent to enable learning etc. These qualities are as important, if not more so, if you have to make people redundant, to hold a difficult performance appraisal, to insist on some level of compliance with company policies and so on.

Here's the rub – as a leader you need to pay more attention to these qualities than those who are not leaders. As I suggested earlier, these behaviours are not at all commonplace in action; you need to be an exemplar of a way of relating which you would like to see taken up throughout your organisation, or that part for which you are responsible.

To recap – leadership is not a cloak which you put on, the attitude and behaviours of a leader to be adopted, a boss who you might be emulating, a set of nostrums about toughness, detachment, being demanding and impatient for results at all costs. This is one of the myths of leadership and it has, in my experience a low success rate in the long run.

I am suggesting that there is a core set of leadership behaviours which are essentially human and right-minded, which as human beings we already know; we do not have to be trained in them but we do have to be reminded of them and be particularly self-aware, paying attention to ways in which, also being human, we tend to fall short. As Warren Bennis said: 'Becoming a leader is synonymous with becoming yourself. It is precisely that simple, and it is also that difficult' (Bennis, 2003).

Reed Hastings, CEO of Netflix, has become well known for creating an extremely successful organisation which is run on radically different principles from most conventional organisations. In two articles in the London *Sunday Times* and *Times* on successive days (Sept 6th and 7th 2020), he talks openly about some lessons he learned from going to marriage guidance counselling. He says 'truth telling improved both marriage and work'. He also learnt the value of acknowledging mistakes and says 'the biggest advantage of *sunshining* a leader's errors is to encourage everyone to think of making mistakes as normal...which leads to greater innovation across the company'.

His comment which has most relevance to this lesson is: 'to be a better leader you have to be a better person', which is saying much the same thing as Bennis. I want to be clear that in quoting Hastings I am not holding up everything that Netflix does as exemplary – it has its shadow side of course, but as Erin Meyer of Insead Business School said, 'there is a lot more to admire than admonish', and it did, in 2018, come second in a 'happiest employment' survey in the US.

It is often argued that it is our very human imperfections which give us the drive and motivation to succeed; our need to prove ourselves, to seek control and power, to win at the expense of others. My colleagues George Binney, Collin Williams and Gerard Wilke, in their excellent book, *Living Leadership* (Binney, 2005) referred to these ego drives as the 'worm' inside. That may well be the case for some leaders, particularly those who strive to reach the very top of their particular tree, but that is no reason why they do not need to treat their subordinates and colleagues well, although there are many examples of those who do not.

LESSON FIVE: YOU ARE WHAT YOU DO

You can infer this lesson from the last one. There are leaders who shout at work, who make demands which are almost impossible to fulfil, who reduce people to tears, who expect their subordinates to work all the hours it takes to get something done.

You have read about them, heard of them, or you may even be such a leader. You may tell yourself that this is acceptable in a stressful work context, and that this is what is necessary to ensure that your priorities are understood and implemented; and you may also tell yourself that in other walks of your life you are fundamentally a good, considerate person, with your family, your friends and your neighbours.

There is an old adage, much beloved by some in the helping profession, that who we are is one thing, and what we do is quite another. This kind of thinking has it that there is some kind of essential self which somehow remains separate from what we do.

But this splitting between being and doing is similar to other splits, such as the split between thinking and doing, or thinking and feeling (head and heart). If you think in this way you would have to see an individual as somehow compartmentalised, with one part being responsible for thinking, one part for feeling, one part for behaving and so forth – and one mysterious part just 'being'! This is an entirely mechanistic view which sees an individual, rather like a car, as comprising a number of parts. This thinking, applied to a human being does not make much sense to me, or to put it more philosophically, seems to be a 'category error'. A 'category error' is when we take the thinking which applies to one ontological category, in this case the category we might call machines, and apply it to an entirely different ontological category, namely the one we call human beings.

When you are shouting at your subordinates, that is who you are, someone who shouts at their subordinates. There is no getting away from it, no justification of saying to yourself 'I am really a nice person, but this situation requires me to behave as a nasty person'. In this situation you are being a nasty person!

I am inviting you to accept another inconvenient truth, and take responsibility for who you are being, even if you don't like yourself:

A while ago, I was a member of the leadership team at Ashridge Consulting (part of Ashridge Business School at the time) and, to put it simply, Ashridge Consulting were not making enough money. We needed a few, larger clients providing us with more substantial assignments. In reviewing what we needed to do differently, we, the leadership team, were told that we were not leading. In the manner rather typical of leadership teams we found this hard to swallow, preferring to locate the problem elsewhere, but we could not escape acknowledging that we were at least part of the problem.

We came up with the rather radical solution that we should refresh and reconstitute the leadership team by our jointly resigning, rethinking the role of the team and inviting applications for re-designed posts. Also, rather typically, there was one person to whom this did not apply, namely the Managing Director, but as he was appointed by the Ashridge governors and we were appointed by him, this was understandable.

I tell you this story for a particular reason; we, the resigning members were also allowed to re-apply for one of these roles (some did and some did not), but each applicant had to solicit feedback from three members of the organisation as to whether they had good reason to apply. I decided to re-apply and duly solicited feedback. I was encouraged to apply because people respected my experience and my reputation in the profession, but I was told that people felt intimidated by me, and that I was quick to dismiss new ideas with which I did not agree.

In short, I was told that I was unaware of how I was using my power and how people often felt silenced by me. I was dismayed; I was showing up in a way that I did not like and did not accord with my self-image; it was painful stuff, but that lesson has stayed with me ever since. Of course, my wife said that she could have told me that without my having to go through such a painful process; this is a bit of a cliché, but I probably would not have taken her seriously – such is the disrespect which familiarity can breed.

THE MYTH OF A SINGULAR AND ENDURING ME

Accepting that you are a nasty person would be a hard pill to swallow if you were to assume that you were just one kind of person, but we all 'show up' differently in different contexts. You will indeed be one kind of person in your family and another, rather different person as a senior executive at work because different contexts evoke different responses. You may find it makes for an easier life to defer to your partner at home, while insisting that your will be done at work. Although different situations evoke different responses and different ways of being, they are all 'you'.

You might think that this sounds rather like having a multiple personality disorder, but there is a crucial difference. Someone with a multiple personality disorder is usually unaware of how they show up differently and what brings on their different 'personalities' (often it is an original trauma). Someone with what we might call a psychosis is fragmented in the sense that each personality has a different story and may even have voices associated with each personality.

The majority of us have some sense of a continuous narrative and history about who we are. What we may lack is an integrating capacity, an awareness of how we show up differently, particularly when some of these ways may not be congruent with our self-image, how we would like to think about ourselves and be seen by others, as in my case. Hence, we use the ways I outlined above, of justifying behaviour of which we may not be too proud, and by telling ourselves that we have no choice, but you **can choose** who you are and how you behave.

There is reasonable evidence to suggest that leaders who do not treat people well, do not create sustainable organisations in the long term. They tend to be better known, perhaps because they make for a better media story. However, there are many highly effective leaders with low profiles, who do not get, or court, publicity, who do, on the whole, treat people well, and you can find many examples of these in, among others, Jim Collins' book, *From Good to Great* (Collins, 2001), and his other book with Jerry Porras, *Built to Last* (Collins, 1994).

IDEAS FOR ACTION

* '360'

  You need to know how people experience you as a leader, what they appreciate and what they might suggest you do differently. The obvious thing is to ask them. The bright idea of '360' occurred to people a long time ago, but then a simple and good idea was turned into an over-engineered mechanism.

  At its worst it takes the form of an elaborate questionnaire, often configured around the company's competency framework. Very often the answers are scored, so the hapless leader receives a raft of numbers and sometimes graphs, which he or she scrolls through anxiously looking for the negatives, but gleans little that he or she can really do much about.

  Better versions have a much freer form which allows contributors to write their responses to three or four simple questions, such as: 'what do you appreciate about X as a leader; what would you like her/him to do differently (more of, less of, start doing, stop doing)'.

  The difficulty is always the subjective nature of such feedback – whether a subordinate feels inhibited by the possibility of being recognised, or takes the opportunity of getting gripes off his chest.

  The best process in my experience is when a third party, often a coach, carries out a face-to-face inquiry among people selected by the leader. Nothing is perfect, but an experienced coach should be able to spot themes and help the leader develop a learning agenda for themselves.

LOOKING FOR THE NEGATIVE

Recently I carried out such an inquiry for a senior Partner in a law firm, and I was most careful to pay a lot of attention to, and amplify what people **appreciated** about him. After we had finished he breathed a visible sigh of relief because he was steeling himself for the negatives. This is another problem with any kind of feedback exercise, that the human being's early brain (reptilian) is programmed to look for danger, and we tend to focus down on the negative and pay little attention to the positive.

- **Your team**, if you lead one, is a very good sounding board about your style and impact, and effective teams need to become skilled at giving each other, including the leader, qualitative feedback. They often need help with this, and I think some kind of team coaching can be very useful; I shall say more about leading teams later.

- Understanding your **'self'**.

In one of my professions as a psychotherapist, there is a great deal written about the nature of the 'self', how people show up in the present moment and how people develop patterns of thinking and behaving; this requires us to think about what we mean by 'self', and what we mean by 'the present moment'. There are many theories and hypotheses on these topics, which I am not intending to cover in this short book on leadership, but there is one that appeals to me and which I think is practical and relevant to leaders.

This is the notion that the 'present moment' is not a static moment, but dynamically emergent. As we act in the present moment we are informed simultaneously by our history and also by our expectations of what is likely to happen next. In other words, the 'present moment' is continuously evolving through cyclical iterations from past to future. If I were to draw it, it would resemble a sort of horizontal spiral.

In practical terms our behaviour 'in the moment' is largely habit; much of the time we are on a kind of auto-pilot, and this is rather useful. You would not want to consider routine movements (routine human proprioception), or how to drive each time you get into your car. However, it might be useful for you to consider your morning work routines, how you plan your day, establish your priorities and so forth.

The most important question I am inviting you to consider is:

* How you handle everyday relational incidents and exigencies – do you *react or respond*?

Transactional Analysis, one of the psychotherapy modalities, has a very practical way of describing human behaviour which they call 'script'. The notion of 'script' suggests that we all have a number of rather habitual ways of thinking and acting which have their origin in what we learnt, observed and experienced with our parents/carers and other early influences. This script we tend to live by serves us well in some circumstances, but scripts developed in childhood will inevitably become obsolete in adulthood, and at worst become an encumbrance if they are maladapted to current circumstances.

* Get to know your 'script'.

Reacting to an incident may well be based on your script. If one of the people who report to you disagrees with you, you may **react** by dismissing his or her point of view. You might even be angry at having your authority challenged. If, however you were to **respond**, that would require you to suspend your immediate reaction and consider what might be a preferable outcome, maybe that your subordinate feels listened to, or that you incorporate their idea into your thinking – something that I, apparently, was singularly failing to do. My father, by the way, was fairly dismissive of my ideas, so this was a behaviour that I was now acting out on my hapless junior colleagues.

I became aware of this when I went into psychotherapy in order to become a better practitioner of Organisational Development.

- Spend some time with a coach.

  You, as a leader, might choose to spend some time with a coach, but the important thing is to become more aware of your reactive tendencies so that you are better able to **respond** proactively and generatively to your colleagues and subordinates.

LETTER THREE:
COMMUNICATION

Dear Leader

How much have you thought about the quality of your communication? You have probably heard a lot about the importance of good communication, but apart from possibly thinking about going on a course to develop your presentation skills, you may not have considered the possibility that 'communicating' is all you really do as a leader, that 'communication' is your main currency. I am going to propose that there are two main kinds of communication. The most obvious kind is associated with the 'formal' aspects of a leader's role, but the more complex and subtle kind is associated with the *informal* aspects of your role, which constitute most of what you do.

Also, I have described the phenomenon of 'organisation' as a *process of communicative interaction*, from which you might infer that a large part of your job, if not the whole of your job, is communicating in one form or another. I intend to unpack and elaborate on, in principle three and its attendant lessons, what I think is involved in 'communicative interaction'.

PRINCIPLE THREE: COMMUNICATION

As I said, this third principle looks, in one sense, obvious, but is much less obvious than it looks. The sociologist George Herbert Mead, as mentioned above, described the process of 'communicative interaction' rather succinctly by saying that 'the meaning of a gesture is in the response' (Mead 1967, p. 146).

He is making a rather radical proposition that communication emerges in the interaction between people, which is a core tenet of the process view of organisations on which I have expanded above. This is very different from the conventionally held view that I can get a message from my head into your head, and that all I have to do is to craft the message well, select the most appropriate medium, and – providing you are disposed to listen well – you will get what I am saying. Mead is saying that, however well the receiver listens, they will 'hear' what you are saying in the context of their 'categories' of knowing.

For example, the concept of 'strategy' might broadly fit into a category which includes vision, mission and tactics, but someone who has been in the forces may well have a different understanding of what it means, from someone who discovered it at business school, or from someone else who has lived through many strategic planning exercises and doubts whether any of them amounted to a 'hill of beans' (as Rick, the world-weary hero put it in the film *Casablanca*). In sum, the views of the person, to whom you are talking about strategy, or anything else, will be conditioned by their experience, their knowledge – what they have read and so forth, and whereas there are likely to be some similarities there are also likely to be significant differences.

Furthermore, how they 'hear' you will be conditioned by their perception of you, how they feel about you, what they imagine might be your unexpressed agenda, not to mention what emotional state they are in on that particular day. So, their meaning will not necessarily be what you intended, and only through dialogue will you come to some shared meaning.

This has profound implications for the practice of leading, the most obvious being that you cannot rely on 'getting the message' out. You will need to convey your intentions, and ideas, and then ask how people are responding to them; you need to iterate between *advocacy and inquiry* with more inquiry than advocacy.

LESSON SIX: LEADERSHIP IS RELATIONAL PRACTICE

What I am proposing from the process view of organisation is that the main currency is 'communicative interaction', mediated of course by its formal arrangements in which participants are shaping and being shaped simultaneously.

Unpacking the term 'communicative interaction', I am suggesting that a leader is always 'relating', directly or indirectly to colleagues, subordinates, or bosses. Explicitly you attend meetings, send emails and so forth, choose which meetings to attend and not attend – not attending is also a relational gesture. Implicitly your subordinates are likely to be aware of your presence as a leader and may have expectations about what you want or don't want, what may please or rile you. The extent to which you are conscious of how you impact, shape and are shaped by this matrix of relating, and how you participate in it, will have a big influence on your effectiveness as a leader.

Expanding a bit further on what I mean by the term 'relational' leadership, the term 'relational' left unexplained, is rather bland – of course leading is relational. What could not be relational about people sitting in a room talking to one another? Life is relational. Heidegger (Heidegger 1978) identifies 'Being-in-the-World-with-Others' as one of the core existential truths, and as Sartre said, 'hell is other people'(Sartre, 1955); like it or not, we cannot easily get away from being in relation to others.

By 'relational' I therefore mean something rather specific, which is not just qualitative. From an existential perspective, we are always in relation to someone or something, as life is inherently relational. We are all made of the same stuff; we are born into a relational context, formed by our primary carers and the milieu into which we are born, and we are, in the broadest sense, interdependent and inter-connected. Even when you are entirely on your own, separate from others in a physical sense, your experience is still relational in that your very ability to state 'I am alone' is only possible because you are able to distinguish different types, or forms of relation. Being in a 'relationship' with another person, is just one form or example of relatedness.

As a leader you might be working with a team or group of others, or you might be on your own, working at your laptop – but you are still in relation in the sense that you have been shaped and influenced by others and are likely to have others in mind as you work. As I sit here, typing away, I am, in a way, acting as a conduit for all those who have influenced me, and am being informed by the myriad conversations in which I have participated over the years, much of which is reiterated and re-created in my head, as my thoughts and ideas evolve in a form of conversation with myself.

As I said, I am not just talking about 'good' relationships, where people observe the social conventions of politeness and consideration, or going further, listen well to one another, taking the ethics of mutual respect, diversity, justice and so forth really seriously. Of course, such ethical principles are important and it is usually important to be polite, although not always.

'Relational leadership' is a shift from the individual-centric perspective which has tended to characterise the discourse about leadership, towards an acknowledgment of the inherently mutual nature of all social process, and therefore prioritising the importance of the co-created, 'here-and-now' relationship as the central medium for influence and transformation.

As I have suggested earlier, what appears to emerge from this process of mutual relating, or what I am calling communicative interaction, is a form of patterning. Complexity scientists, as I described above, think this arises from an inherent tendency for *self-organisation* to emerge in nature and all social processes; a form of order, but one which cannot be predicted, except in the very short term, and in which a particular effect cannot be traced to a single cause.

In the short term, routine work takes place in a more or less predictable way, but if the longer term is so unpredictable, it raises a tricky question for leaders about the basis on which to initiate action.

My contention, that leadership is a relational practice which arises between people in an on-going negotiation of mutual influence, albeit within a framework of formal authority, requires a shift from a mindset wherein employees are entirely dependent on leaders to make decisions, inform, and motivate (power over), to a more mutual interdependence (power with), in which both parties participate in an empowered process.

In general, I am suggesting that the leader's role is to orchestrate and enable, to mobilise the organisation's collective intelligence, while followers have to choose to take initiative and responsibility within a framework of organisational intent, expressed overall in its purpose, policy and strategy, and by you in your local context.

Specifically, I think there are three particular implications for you as a leader:

- The first is that conversation is the main currency in organisations, so how you *engage* in and shape the continuous conversation, which is the stuff of organisational life, is what really matters.
- The second is that you do this by convening conversations around issues or questions you think need addressing; that means bringing people together who might have some interesting contributions as well as people who are likely to play a part in making something happen.
- The third is that you need to create specific forms to address particular issues or problems, such as task or project groups, and often this means going beyond your immediate reports and working across silos, functions and departments – this may trouble some people, but it is how innovation is most likely to happen.

LESSON SEVEN: THE FOLLY OF UTOPIAN SOLUTIONS

Grand Utopian solutions like the roll-out of value programmes, or cultural change programmes, are rarely an answer to anything, except to satisfy some people that you are doing something. A 'programme' of change, or leadership development, is easier to set up for leaders in the sense that it appears as a tangible project with costs attached to stages and time lines, but it is usually an off-the-shelf type of solution to a more complex problem which is either too hard, too scary or too difficult to address.

'IF YOU WANT TO CHANGE, FOCUS ON WHAT IS'

I was asked to help a UK local authority with a culture change, and I brought in my colleague Patricia Shaw to work with me. The exact nature of the required cultural change was never clearly stated, which we saw as an advantage. The Council had recently turned Labour (the UK socialist party) after years of Conservative domination, and we presumed the new members wanted to be seen to be making a difference, and put themselves in a stronger electoral position. The old regime had become extremely complacent, slow to adapt to the winds of change in local government, and as it turned out, somewhat corrupt. The place was run a little bit like a gentleman's club, and the servants were treated accordingly

Change consultants were sought, preferably a male and female, and preferably independent. We understood that other consultants in the competitive tendering process had proffered elaborate methodologies for diagnosing and then changing culture, whereas we offered a view based on the principle I outlined in in lesson one. Essentially, we said that culture was not a 'thing' which could be diagnosed, but was continuously emerging in the ongoing process of 'communicative interaction'. The CEO responded well to what we proposed, and we were appointed on the basis of a submission which outlined an **inquiry** methodology of **engaging with** the culture.

The starting point of our methodology was unusual because we asked if we could just come into the organisation and start meeting and talking to people. We called this initial inquiry method 'wandering around' and we combined 'wandering around', with personal interviews with all the members of the Executive Management Team and a few other 'key players'.

Our assignment was announced by a letter from the CEO, explaining the essence of the work and that people might encounter us, and asking people to collaborate with us. In a sense it was a legitimising letter. We had explained that we did not want to do a set-piece diagnosis, but instead wanted to encounter people in their work context, hence wandering around – turning up with our identification badges, finding a place to start our enquiry and seeing where it led us. Patricia Shaw, my work partner and an extrovert in the Myers Briggs sense, found this process much easier than I did!

We then decided to put a small piece of structure around our method by putting an announcement in the house magazine, reminding people of what we were doing and inviting them to come and talk to us if they were interested in what we were doing, wanted to see some change, and had some energy for taking an active part. We gave six dates and times, found a large room with tea and biscuits, and waited. The Personnel Director told us no one would come because arrangements had not been made with management, but we stuck to our guns.

Eight people turned up to the first meeting, four to the second and eighteen to the third, and eighteen or so to subsequent meetings. Word got around that we were actually wanting to listen! We were focusing on 'what is', namely people's lived experience of what it was like to go on together in this organisation. Later we brought together large groups of seventy to eighty people, to continue this conversation, which generated considerable excitement and energy for change, and not surprisingly, some less than appreciative responses from senior managers, but that is a story for another book.

LESSON EIGHT: HOW TO MAKE 'HIGH-PROFILE', COMMUNICATIVE GESTURES

I have been proposing that communication is a non-linear reciprocal process, characterised by an almost simultaneous iteration of gesture and response in which meaning emerges in complex interaction, and I have elaborated on some of the implications of this perspective. Now I intend to talk about a more familiar and practical aspect of communication, which, as I said at the beginning of this letter, is associated with the more formal aspects of your role.

As I suggested, there are, I think, broadly two kinds of communicative gesture, and another way of characterising them which I have borrowed from Edgar Schein (Schein, 1992), is as 'high-profile' and 'low-profile' gestures. The 'high-profile' gestures are those which you make towards a large number of people at the same time, for example a 'town-hall' type of meeting, or the launching of some major initiative. 'Low profile' gestures are the everyday encounters, team meetings, emails and so forth, and many of the above lessons have focused on your 'low-profile' gestures as you participate, as a leader, in responding to and shaping the social process which constitutes organisational life. Often, too much attention is paid to the leader's ability to make 'high-profile' gestures, because it is in the everyday encounters that people discover who you really are as a leader.

But I do want to pay some attention to the high-profile gestures which all leaders are required to make from time to time, because they can be of great symbolic significance, and they tend to generate some anxiety in many leaders, who worry about whether they have the necessary skills. You do not need to be a great orator or wordsmith, but you need to pay attention to the quality of this particular type of communicative gesture; it needs to be clear, direct, concise and engaging. I want to take each of these in turn:

- *Clarity* comes through the use of fairly simple language, which is not cloaked in business jargon. Avoid over-used, clichéd phrases such as 'going forward', 'drilling down', 'touch base offline', 'singing from the same hymn sheet' and so forth. We have all heard them, and not only are most of them more or less meaningless, they are not personal, so your listeners do not know whether this is **you** speaking, or whether you are quoting from a corporate script.

- *Direct* speaking comes, rather obviously, in face-to-face contexts, from looking people in the eye. It is however surprising how leaders often appear transfixed by their notes, avoid answering questions directly and spontaneously, and sometimes even avoid taking questions. They feel the need to 'stick to the script' and fear getting drawn into areas where they do not have a ready answer.

Bill Clinton was known for his capacity to speak directly to people; apparently when he was giving an address, people in the room had the sense that he was speaking directly to them. Of course, he was a highly accomplished politician, and this was a particular skill he had honed, but I think he was willing to give 'in the moment' responses to questions, being unafraid of not having a ready answer.

To give a more corporate example, I once ran a 'strategy' event for a company, at which there were around eighty people in the room, grouped into regional teams. My intention was to minimise presentations and optimise conversation. A short presentation was made on each section of the strategy, offering options and questions to be addressed. I suggested having members of the executive team dispersed among the regions, to listen to their responses to the questions raised, and then having the executive team meet in the middle of the room to share what they had heard and explore their responses.

When I first proposed this, a member of the executive team was incredulous: 'You mean you want us to respond without leaving the room and discussing our response first, and getting our act together?' 'That's exactly what I mean,' I replied. Fortunately, the Chief Executive was intrigued by the notion, and that is what they did, and it went down as one of the best strategy events they had ever had.

What I was encouraging was spontaneity and a sense of 'thinking together', rather than 'exchanging pre-thoughts' which is what most executive meetings tend to consist of.

- *Concise.* There is an apocryphal story of Mozart being told by Emperor Joseph 11, after a performance of his latest opera, 'too many notes, my dear Mozart' or something similar. Mozart responded that there were 'exactly as many as are necessary', but this is not always the case with leaders' speeches or presentations. Too often, the use of too many words betrays an absence of real substance.

- *Engaging.* Everything I have said before applies, but there is something important to add. I think that there are two forms of speaking, an explanatory form and an expressive form. The explanatory form, as the word implies, attempts to explain something cognitively, and as such appeals to our cognitive processes. The expressive form, however, is designed to appeal to our feelings, and is the quality most likely to engage people.

It is somewhat intangible, and as I am writing during the recent coronavirus lockdown, it is hard not to use a recent example from the British Queen, who rarely speaks to the whole population, except at Christmas. But her brief talk seemed to have an extraordinary impact, was watched extensively beyond British shores and seemed to provide a sense of hope and comfort. My own sense was that she wrote it herself; I imagine she had some help, but it felt personal – they seemed to be her words. Clearly, she was not telling us about Covid-19; we had all heard enough about that already, so it was mainly an expressive form, and the more powerful it was for that.

The lesson here is that your team or your organisation wants to hear from you. They want to feel that you are levelling with them, and they don't want to be fobbed off with a corporate script. They want to hear what you know, what you don't know, and what you are thinking of doing, and they appreciate being asked for their views; they are sensible enough to know that you can't incorporate every-one's views into your decisions, but they want to feel heard.

VIRTUAL COMMUNICATION

I think I need to say something about virtual communication as it seems likely that we shall continue to use virtual platforms for at least some of the time. I don't think it changes anything in the principle that I have outlined, but it does raise some interesting issues. I have conducted many coaching, supervision and therapy sessions, and I have also facilitated three Board workshops, the most difficult of which concerned the dynamics of a team.

I found the one-to-one meetings quite straightforward, but I had never expected to facilitate a meeting about a group's interpersonal dynamics virtually, and initially insisted that we wait until we could meet face to face. However, as time was of the essence, I agreed to do it virtually and I would say it worked partially. Here are some of my brief reflections:

+ Meetings have hitherto taken place in the office, but in virtual meetings we see into people's houses which, for some, constitutes some kind of invasion into their personal space. As I have repeated throughout this book, context is important as it changes how we make sense of situations and the people in them, so seeing someone in their home office, their kitchen, dining room or in some cases their car, makes a difference to our perception of individuals. People respond differently to being seen in this way; for those who tend to be introverted it may be uncomfortable while others enjoy the informality, but it suggests that you as a leader need give thought to what you imagine people will make of what they can see, what your context may convey about you. The pictures on the wall behind you, whether you have changed out of your running kit and so forth, are likely to be noticed, but probably not referred to. For some people a child running into the room is endearing, while for others it is a distraction. The meeting in the car suggested that my client did not want to be overheard, and I have been in meetings where my client was constantly looking around, clearly feeling inhibited by the possibility of being overheard or interrupted by someone with whom they were sharing their living space.

• Real team dialogue is difficult enough in face-to-face situations and even more so virtually. What I mean by 'real' dialogue is when people **respond** to one another, and a flow develops which builds to some agreed view or decision; differences are expressed, but people listen and acknowledge each other's views and feelings. On a screen it is quite hard to experience how others are responding to you, particularly when there is something being displayed on a shared screen, and one of the reasons for this is the absence of **resonance.**

• This is for me, the most serious deficit of virtual communication. There is a fair amount of evidence that human bodies 'resonate' with one another. We can sense in our bodies how someone is responding to us; we literally sense the response of another body when we pay them our full attention. We may not know what name the person will put to their emotional response, but we can sense something going on, maybe pleasure, anger, anxiety, but at least we sense enough to inquire. I think this is the neurophysiological base of empathy, and it seems likely that this dimension will be missing in virtual communication, thereby impoverishing the potential richness of intimate exchange.

There is much more to be said about virtual communication, and while there is plenty of speculation on its impact, no-one really knows how, post-Covid-19, it is going to shape the nature of organisational life. I have two general concerns, one being that as humans are a naturally social species which thrives on contact, such an impoverishment, if it were to become a new norm, would not be good for organisation wellbeing.

My second concern is about innovation. I think we are learning that much of our day-to-day business can be conducted virtually, but, in view of what I have already said about the conditions which foster innovation, such as experimentation, initiative, some degree of conflict and mess, I am not sure that virtual communication – which needs to fairly structured and ordered – provides such conditions. We shall see.

IDEAS FOR ACTION

• Find someone who will be your 'critical friend' and tell you how you come across when you communicate, in whatever media you tend to use.

• If you are someone who has to give presentations, ask a professional to sit in and give you feedback. For example, I had to give a series of presentations to groups of eighty people and I asked someone who specialised in presentations to give me feedback. I thought I was quite good at public speaking as it was part of my job, but my illusions were seriously disturbed. I tended to start in a rather tentative and self-deprecating way in an effort to invite participation and not come over as too much of an expert, but she pointed out that eighty people had given up much of their morning to come to this session, and wanted to be assured that it was going to be at least interesting and possibly useful, and that in my opening I needed to appear confident and quickly demonstrate that I knew what I was talking about. My style of making presentations, particularly the opening part, was changed for ever.

Later I came across Patsy Rodenburg, voice coach at the Guildhall school for over thirty years. She introduced me to her 'three circles' (Rodenburg, 2007). In her top circle one is trying to assert one's confidence over one's audience; in the bottom circle, where I was, one comes across as too self-deprecating. The sweet spot is in what she calls the 'second circle', where one speaks confidently to people, being neither overly humble nor over-confident or self-important.

LESSON NINE: NEVER MAKE AN IMPORTANT DECISION ON YOUR OWN

The first part of this lesson, which I referred to earlier as one of W.L. Gore's principles, can be inferred from most of what has gone before. If you are a participant in a complex and continuously emerging social process, of which no one is in control, and to which no one person can have 'the answer', and yet you have to make decisions and act into inevitable uncertainty, it makes no sense whatever to make important decisions on your own; this is the riskiest move you can make.

Some leaders, conditioned in the high-testosterone, macho school of leadership, think they are expected to make decisions on their own; that not doing so would be a sign of weakness. In my view, not consulting some valued colleagues and peers would be a sign of stupidity. Where there is no one 'truth', but a multiplicity of perspectives and experiences, the least you can do is to consult peers and colleagues; the best you could do is to arrive at some degree of consensus on the best course of action with your own team, on which more later.

I am not suggesting that you form a committee or task force every time you have a decision to make, but I am suggesting you consult as widely as possible in the time available. Sometimes a consensus will emerge, and at other times you will have to act into what seems to be emerging. Leaders don't make decisions so much as decisions are waiting to be taken; often the need for a decision is obvious to most people around you, although there may well be many different views on what the decision needs to be. You need to explore these perspectives, and at best you will discover a fair amount of common ground, but here's the thing; you will need the courage to actually take a decision, despite the fact that a few people's noses may be put out of joint. This is what leaders have to do.

'LETTING IT EMERGE'

As creator and leader of the Ashridge Masters in Organisation Consulting, I had chosen a faculty to design and deliver
the programme. It was a two-year programme with a number
of workshops to deliver, learning group leaders were needed
as were supervision supervisors and dissertation assessors. In
addition, we were being encouraged to open up the faculty to
other members of Ashridge staff and increase diversity. It was
a fairly high-profile and controversial programme within the
business school

Because of the highly distributed nature of authority among
faculty, I was beginning to sense we were at risk of losing
the integrity and quality of the programme, and because the
whole faculty participated in the programme management
meetings, I was starting to feel the size made it unwieldy, and –
to paraphrase W.B. Yeats – the centre was not holding.

I consulted my boss, the MD of Ashridge Consulting, and
he advised me to simply choose my smaller programme
management team and inform people. It felt simple but rather
authoritarian, and possibly arbitrary. I consulted another
colleague and she suggested I have one-on-one conversations with all members of faculty, articulating what I saw
as the problem, and that I needed a smaller team, and see
what emerged. I chose that approach, and to my amazement
everyone saw the problem and the solution, and people
variously declared their interest in being part of the team or
otherwise. The solution emerged; it wasn't quite what I had
anticipated or ideally wanted, but it was good enough, and the
process felt inclusive.

LETTER FOUR:
YOUR TEAM

Dear Leader

What is your relationship with your own team, and how well does it work, *as a team?*

PRINCIPLE FOUR: TEAMS AND TEAMWORKING

One of the most obvious sets of people to consult will be your team. It is something of a truism that choosing and developing your team is one of the most important tasks you have. Unfortunately, team working in modern, functionally designed organisations does not come easily, particularly, as most western organisations are predicated on an engineering assumption about the importance of each part performing effectively.

Combine this deep-rooted assumption with the fact that most people rise to the top of their departments because they are experts in a particular function – be it planning, marketing, operations, distribution and so on – so their function or department tends to take precedence over the group in terms of their identification with that function, their knowledge of it and their reward for its effective management.

Furthermore, departmental heads find themselves as de facto members of the 'executive team' without any real sense of team purpose or commitment to it. Many team meetings are little more than rituals or forums for communication. So, although much lip service is paid to the importance of teamwork, the reality is that many managers have few conceptual frameworks or models for thinking about what conditions might lead to effective top teamwork.

To address this reality, a colleague, David Casey, and I, having done a great deal of work with executive teams, wrote an article called 'Second Thoughts on Team Building' (Critchley, 1984), and I intend to draw on this in this lesson.

LESSON TEN: DEVELOPING YOUR TEAM

David and I had run a number of 'teambuilding' sessions with top management groups and we were becoming professionally identified with this sort of work. However, we were beginning to have some 'second thoughts' about what we were doing. We began to doubt whether, for most of their time, these groups of people really needed to work as the sort of team we were advocating. We began to consider the possibility, like so many consultants, that maybe we had a solution in search of a problem!

We acknowledged that we had both been working from some implicit assumptions that good teamwork is characterised by high levels of openness, trust and sharing, and that such teamwork is a characteristic of healthy, effectively functioning organisations. We assumed that our primary job was to foster and develop what has come to be referred to as 'emotional intelligence'. We then started to face up to an awkward reality that our solution was like the proverbial shotgun; not all teams really needed to be teams, and most teams do not need particularly high levels of emotional intelligence to function 'well enough'.

Taking one example of a local authority, it became apparent that the Director of Education had little need to work in close harmony with his fellow chief officers, who had neither the expertise, the interest, nor indeed the time, to contribute to what is essentially very specialised work, and vice versa.

In industry, whilst it is clear that the marketing and production directors of a company must work closely together to ensure that the production schedule is synchronised with sales forecasts, and the finance director needs to be involved to look at the cash flow implications of varying stock levels and so forth, they don't need to involve the whole team. And they certainly do not need to develop high levels of trust and openness to work through those kinds of business issues.

On the other hand, most people would agree that strategic decisions, concerned with the future direction of the whole enterprise, should involve all those at the top. Strategy should demand an input from every member of the top group, and for strategic discussion and strategic decision-making, teamwork at the top is essential.

But how much time do most top management groups actually spend discussing strategy? Our experiences, in a wide variety of organisations, suggest that 10% is a high figure for most organisations – often 5% would be nearer the mark. This means that 90–95% of decisions in organisations are essentially operational; that is decisions made within departments based, usually, on a fair amount of information and expertise. In those conditions, high levels of emotional intelligence may be nice, but not necessary; consensus is strictly not an issue, and in any case would take up far too much time. There is therefore no need for high levels of interpersonal skills.

We then concluded that the most important starting point for you the leader, is to get very clear about what kind of tasks can only be accomplished by the 'senior team' being **in the room together and at the same time**. Interestingly this question is rarely addressed. The team comes together because it assumes it is supposed to; a routine agenda is created and circulated by the PA to the boss, and people leave most meetings feeling that they have just wasted half a day.

The following framework (Critchley, 1984) is an effective starting point to clarify your team's purpose and mode of operating:

A model showing executive team roles and 'modes' of working

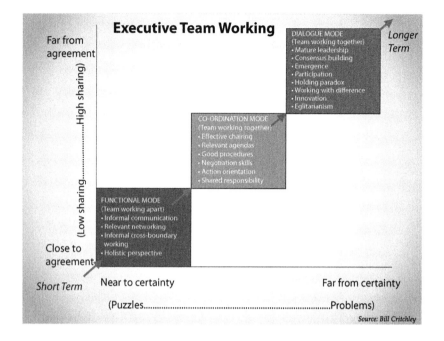

Source: Bill Critchley

This framework (Critchley, 1984) is an effective starting point to clarify an executive team's purpose and mode of operating. This model works on the assumption that most actual work is carried out in functions and is subject to functional expertise. Much of the work is of the 'puzzle' variety, where solutions are discovered through the application of expertise. Some of these 'puzzles' are more complex and require inter-departmental collaboration and have to be co-ordinated, and then there are the 'strategic' problems, which are not subject to expertise, but need to be thoroughly discussed until some solution emerges by common consent. This framework is based on a distinction made by Reg Revans (Revans, 1965) between puzzles and problems, and since then a variety of similar distinctions have been made, for example the notion of 'wicked problems' (Camillus, 2008). I shall now summarise the main implications of the framework:

1. Unshared Certainty (functional mode, bottom left) – puzzles are simple and operational; there is no need to share with the wider group. Decisions are taken within the

functional area. Many teams devote too much time to these functional issues to the frustration of everyone.

2. Co-operation (co-ordination mode, middle) – puzzles are more complex and require sharing of ideas, approaches and decision-making. This kind of operational co-ordination needs discipline and effective chairing.

3. Shared Uncertainty (dialogue mode, top right) – this is the domain of the **strategic** decision and other such problems where a high degree of sharing is required to overcome obstacles of personal agendas, function protection, risk aversion and so forth. Attachment to the known and know-able is replaced with group responsibility for entering into the unknown with the combined knowledge, expertise and wisdom of the whole group.

Effectiveness in the third mode is hard to reach, because maturity and a high level of 'emotional intelligence' is required.

For a management team to function optimally requires the team to recognise these distinctions, to take off its agenda all functional items (mode 1), develop an effective and disciplined approach to mode 2, and to develop the dialogic skills to be effective in mode 3.

The main challenge for individuals is that they have to learn to leave their functional hats behind when they join a management or corporate team and step up to a **collective leadership role**. This will require them to venture out of their comfort zone to engage in sometimes difficult conversations about other functional areas, to make trade-offs and compromises in service of the overall good, and to become involved in the leadership of the whole organisation.

Most people find choice and uncertainty uncomfortable. Many senior managers attempt to deny the choice element by the employ-ment of complex models and techniques. Most people's management experience, and much management education puts the main emphasis on establishing as many facts as possible and reviewing options in the light of past experience. That's why such models are so popular. They provide comforting analytic frameworks for looking at strategic options, and they are appealing to our need to create certainty out of uncertainty. The hope is that they will magic up a solution to the strategic question. But of course, they can't make choices for people and they don't throw any light on the future.

The top team of an organisation, if it is to achieve quality and commitment in its decisions about future directions, will need to pool the full extent of each individual's wisdom and experience. That means something quite different from reacting to a puzzle in terms of their own functional knowledge and experience. It means exposing fully their uncertainties, taking unaccustomed risks by airing their own subjective view of the world and struggling to build some common perceptions and possibilities.

This is where that over-used word 'sharing' really comes into its own. In this context it is not merely a value-laden exhortation, it is vital to the future of the organisation. Ideas and opinions are all we have to inform our view of the future, but if we are to take a risk with a fragile idea or opinion informed by intuition and experience, but unsubstantiated by 'facts', we will take it only if the climate is right. Conversely, if we take the risk, and the 'out of the box' nature, or vulnerability of the idea elicits a volley of ridicule and abuse, then it will die on the instant, lost forever, snuffed out like Tinkerbell.

Most functional executives, brought up in the hurly-burly of politics and inter-functional warfare, find the transition from functional to strategic mode very difficult to make. They do not always see the difference, and if they do, they are reluctant to leave their mountain top, the summit of knowledge, experience and hence power, for the quality and shared uncertainty of creative problem-solving, often in the form of strategic decision-making. And yet this is the one area where real teamwork is not only necessary, but vital.

THE ROLE OF THE LEADER

In the mode of *unshared certainty*, the leader is rarely needed at all, indeed the 'team' probably does not need to meet in a team.

This form of puzzle-solving is largely achieved within functions, at informal cross-functional meetings, or in task groups.

In the mode of *co-operation*, the leader's role is well established in management convention as the 'Chair'. This kind of meeting, often known as 'SMT' or the 'ops' meeting, is usually held monthly or more frequently. They need to be focused, disciplined and often quite short. The chair is responsible for ensuring there is a clear and relevant (items which are of concern to most team members) agenda, and maintaining the discipline needed to get through the agenda. This role requires considerable skill in managing the process, such as keeping the discussion to the point, curtailing over-dominant members, or ramblers, while enabling all members to have sufficient input, and for converging the discussion to a conclusion.

THE MODE OF SHARED UNCERTAINTY

In this mode the leader is more of a facilitator than a Chair, and indeed teams often rotate this role depending on the topic under discussion. For example, if the topic were to be a review of senior talent and succession, the HR director might lead it.

The main challenge in this mode, apart from whether or not all members are willing or not to leave their mountain top and seriously engage, is whether the leader is really up for it, as it involves some dilution of his/her authority. The reason for making this move is because research suggests that such a shared responsibility produces higher quality and more sustainable strategic decisions in the long run, but it requires a high level of maturity on behalf of all team members and particularly the leader.

In public companies Directors are legally responsible for the management of a company's business and ensuring that it meets its statutory obligations. In other types of organisations, such as subsidiaries of corporations, privately owned, or public sector organisations, the same principle applies, but it may require the CEO to demand the same level of collective responsibility. In such cases it represents a dilution of the unalloyed individual responsibility and accountability of the CEO, to a shared responsibility, even though the CEO remains as the executive accountable for the performance of the whole enterprise. Thus, the CEO is sharing his or her responsibility while retaining ultimate accountability. This is apparently paradoxical but it is also, I think, what CEOs are paid to do.

Team members are usually judged on their performance in their functional role, and rarely for the way they perform as an Executive team. It may well be more comfortable for them to keep things this way and leave the burden of the whole enterprise to the CEO. However, I think stepping up to collective responsibility is a demand a leader can, and should make, and has often been the main purpose of bringing me in as a facilitator.

POSSIBLE ACTIONS TO DEVELOP YOUR TEAM

There are a number of topics that you might need to cover as part of a team development project, such as:

- Establishing the purpose of being a team: what is it the team needs to do together? In practice this often leads to agreement about a broad agenda, which might cover items like strategy, structure, succession planning, people development, performance management etc.

- What structure of meetings is needed? For example, some teams have regular, short operational meetings (mode 2), and less frequently, more 'strategic' meetings (mode 3), where they give themselves time to reflect and discuss the longer term, more complex issues. Teams have found this framework very helpful in enabling them to identify their different purposes and hence the need for different kinds of meeting.

- How are they going to work together effectively as a team in the different modes? Mode 2 requires a team to develop 'good enough' interpersonal communication, while mode 3 demands the skills of **dialogue**, where understanding something about team dynamics might be helpful, e.g. power dynamics in teams, the dynamics of inclusion and exclusion, to mention but two. There are some simple frameworks for thinking about these kinds of dynamics, which might inform the dimensions of teamworking to be explored, and any experienced team coach should be able to provide them. However, do be wary of over-elaborate models which purport to diagnose team functioning. The best use of models is when they are used lightly, to provoke conversation, and they should not, in my view, be used as interpretative tools. I do think some people in my profession tend to over-rely on them.

• Team roles: people are inclined to take up particular roles in teams, and it is useful to become aware of these habitual roles, their effects and how to develop flexibility.

• Team leadership: leaders need to develop the skill of facilitating and enabling consensus decisions within clear boundaries.

LETTER FIVE:
A QUESTION OF PURPOSE

Dear Leader

What is your purpose? Do you have a personal purpose, or do you take it for granted that it is your job to fulfil the organisation's purpose? If you do have a sense of personal purpose, do you see it in purely financial terms, or does it extend beyond financial goals? My next principle explores the crucial role of purpose.

PRINCIPLE FIVE: PURPOSE AS THE FOUNDATION OF ALL ACTION

A recent study by the Chartered Institute of Personnel and Development and the High Pay Centre in the UK found that executive bonuses are skewed to financial targets with no, or very little weighting given to the wellbeing, training and engagement of staff. Over the entire FTSE 100, employee metrics accounted for two percent of bonus weighting while financial targets accounted for eighty-two percent. These financial metrics include items like total shareholder return, return on capital, earnings per share and measures of cash flow and sales. You will probably be familiar with this focus on financial return and enhancing shareholder value, and you may well have been taught that maximising shareholder value is the overriding purpose of a commercial organisation and hence your primary responsibility.

It is self-evident that people form organisations for some *purpose* which requires a form of collective endeavour, and the post-enlightenment, classical liberal economic model, promulgated in particular by economists like Friedman and Hayek, stated that free markets are perfectly efficient, and that ruthless focus on these ends, achieved by maximising shareholder value, brings efficiency and innovation, and co-ordinates millions of firms to meet the needs of billions of people.

Unfortunately, it is becoming apparent that this preoccupation with enhancing shareholder value is no longer sustainable. It is not my intention to write a polemic on the flaws of the prevailing capitalist model, but Rebecca Henderson (Henderson, 2020) makes a compelling case for 'reimagining capitalism'. She acknowledges that the prevailing model has given rise to considerable growth but that the environmental costs of this growth have remained largely invisible, as companies have seen them as 'externalities' for which they are not responsible. Alongside this growth has come the emergence of global capitalism where many prices are wildly 'out of whack' as she puts it, as global firms fix the rules of the game in their favour, using their power and political influence. She suggests that we are probably paying only about 40% of the real costs of fossil fuels, and this distortion caused by the failure to price GHG emissions, is enormous.

If you are asking yourself, 'what has this got to do with me?', the answer is it has a lot to do with all leaders, and I am arguing that it requires you to see profit as a necessary condition of fulfilling what Henderson refers to as 'shared value', but not as an end it itself, and certainly not the only one.

She describes this as 'a move from a world in which environmental and social capital are essentially free (or someone else's business), to a world in which the need to operate within environmental limits within a thriving society is taken for granted'. She says this requires us to build 'purpose-driven organisations', and this is where you come in.

In my experience these questions about purpose are sometimes asked, but mainly not asked, namely, 'What are we here for? What are we doing together? How do we make sense of the amount of time we spend 'working'?' So, I am inviting you to ask these questions, of yourself but also of the organisations of which you are a part. There are always personal answers to these questions, such as those at the bottom of Maslow's famous hierarchy of needs, earning the money to pay the rent, or at the higher end, to achieve status or fulfilment (Maslow, 1954).

Although the personal purposes for people of working age are many and various, I think people usually expect, and are motivated by, a sense of what this organisation, or my part of the organisation is here for, or what is the purpose of this project. I think it is part of a leader's role to enable people to make meaning of their work through rigorously posing these questions.

Many organisations have indeed addressed such questions by developing elaborate mission or vision statements, but they are often so generic, or lofty, that they are hard for individuals to relate to, and any questions of purpose in relation to the environment or society are usually conspicuous by their absence. For example, take two 'goliaths'. Amazon's is: 'To be Earth's most customer-centric company, where customers can find and discover anything they might want to buy online'. I wonder whether this gives meaning to a supervisor in an Amazon warehouse, going home exhausted. Nike's is: 'Bring inspiration and innovation to every athlete in the world. If you have a body, you are an athlete'. Again, I wonder how much meaning this brings to the life of someone working in a Nike factory.

This question of purpose abounds in buzz words, like 'mission', 'vision', 'strategic goals', and sometimes 'values' is thrown in too. Appended to such words is another over-used construct, 'strategy', and firms of consultants have made a great deal of money writing about them, and helping companies to craft impressive statements which can be communicated to the waiting staff. But, as Macbeth put it, these statements are usually 'full of sound and fury, signifying nothing'. For some reasons, a kind of business language has evolved, containing all sorts of lofty phrases and clichés which merely serve to obfuscate and obscure. I think this may have been with the rise of what was known as 'scientific management', and a language was needed which sounded serious and scientific, or because managers wanted to join the ranks of the professions.

In my view management is neither a science nor a profession, but a **practice**, and it is a practice, as I have been saying, largely concerned with communicating, and it helps if leaders communicate in accessible and meaningful language. I suggest that there are three simple questions to which leaders need to provide some answers in the quest for purpose:

- What are we doing (this is what is usually meant by mission)?
- Why are we doing it (this is what is usually meant by purpose)?
- How are we going to do it (this is what is broadly meant by strategy)?

These are simple questions, and it helps to put them in simple terms, but answering them is not so easy.

For example, what am I doing? The easy answer is 'writing a book', but that is the wrong answer. My intention is to convey my experience and think about what leadership **really** is, as opposed to what it is supposed to be.

Why am I doing it? For a number of reasons; I think if more leaders were to follow these principles and lessons, organisations would be better places to work in, more sustainable in the broadest sense of the word, more responsive and innovative, and more effective (a bit grandiose you might say, but I really do aspire to that). And there is some ego involved in the sense that my personal purpose is to make a difference to how people live their lives; I get a real buzz when I have helped someone or some team to make a real shift in the way they think and operate.

How am I going to do it? Well, at the time of writing I think that getting a book published is the way to do it, but that could change when I go to meet my publisher!

These really are important questions.

LESSON 11: FINDING PURPOSE

The following example illustrates the importance of 'finding purpose', but it also reprises suggestions from lesson seven, 'the folly of Utopian solutions', and reasserts the principle of working from 'what is'. The paradoxical theory of change (Beisser, 1970) suggests that change emerges through heightening awareness of what is going on in the present. It is both paradoxical and counter-intuitive, because most managers assume, and most change programmes are predicated on describing a 'vision' of a future desired state, and then building a programme of change activities which takes an organisation towards this desired state. However, for many reasons which I have already given, this deductive, rather engineered approach, rarely if ever gives rise to the desired outcome. Instead, by working **inductively** from where we are now, the issues which need to be addressed become clear, and change activities can be configured around them. My final case study is an illustration of such a change process.

In this vignette, the 'what' was fairly clear. The firm were management consultants providing consulting services along fairly conventional lines, such as finance, business strategy, HR etc. The 'how' was more or less clear, but they felt that what was missing was a shared sense of purpose and values.

They asked Patricia Shaw and I to help them develop a 'a set of values'. They had been growing fast and wanted, as they put it 'to get back to their values' which they thought they had lost as they grew. This organisation was spawned by one of the accounting practices and was in its first stage of rapid growth. Senior management spoke nostalgically of the time when, as a smaller organisation, they experienced a sense of shared values, and of their desire to recapture that lost state. They expected us to help them create a value statement, which they then intended to communicate and 'roll out' to the rest of the organisation. Before they appointed consultants, they had hired a large London venue for a date, some six weeks from the start of the work, at which they intended to 'launch' the new company values. The 'Utopian' purpose of creating a set of shared values was to 'align their culture with their strategic goals', and it was when 'values-led' change was the fad of the time.

As is so often the case with major change initiatives of the Utopian variety, management assumes that employees can be persuaded to follow a newly minted set of values by a mixture of exhortation and 'effective communication'. All that is needed is to come up with the 'right' set of values, and this is what we had been hired to do. As I relate this story, I am wondering whether the belief that a set of value statements, crafted by senior managers with the aid of some consultants, to serve in some way to unite a diverse set of consulting practices, and provide some coherence to a growing and entrepreneurial business, makes sense to you? It is an approach to culture change which still has some currency.

For it to make sense, one would have to assume that a large group of intelligent and resourceful employees will believe what their senior management tells them to believe, or at least, that they will behave as if they do. It certainly seems doubtful to me, and yet this was, and still is a very common expectation.

I worked with Patricia Shaw, a colleague of mine with whom I had obtained my Diploma in Gestalt in organisations, and we managed to persuade our immediate clients of an approach based on the Gestalt 'paradoxical theory of change' which I introduced above, and, unsurprisingly, you may well notice some methodological similarities to my earlier account of our work with the Local Authority.

We embarked on an *inquiry* into their **currently enacted** values, by talking to all the partners, and then by bringing them together to reflect on what was emerging, what they could infer about the 'culture' they were sustaining. They were somewhat shocked by our approach, and the MD was at first angry with us, because, as he put it, he had spent a year trying to 'put a lid on all this stuff', and he initially wanted to put a stop to our work. However, I was able to persuade him, without using these exact words, that the problem with 'Utopian' solutions is that they try to ignore 'this stuff', namely people's lived experience and realities, and hence they mainly tend to give rise to cynicism.

As it turned out, this group of partners were able to engage in a rather humbling conversation as they remembered their own experiences of being treated as bag carriers, and put through rather humiliating newcomer rituals when they first joined the organisation. They realised that they were, to some extent perpetuating similar experiences among junior staff. Faced with this acknowledgment of what was really happening in the present, they resolved to make some changes which would **later** be enshrined in value statements.

One supposed appeal of a set of values is that it should provide a behavioural framework, a set of 'rules', part ethical and part practical, which will inform, and therefore limit the diversity of micro-interactions in the service of creating some harmony and consistency. This is one aspiration which arises from an adaptation of Darwinian theory, embedded in the predominant management discourse, that 'fitness' for survival requires consistency of behaviour upheld by shared values, configured around a set of well-articulated strategic goals. As I have explained earlier, such 'alignment' is conceived as a requisite for competitive success. Our clients feared fragmentation, having previously experienced cohesion, and it was this sense of cohesion and consistency which they sought to re-create.

The second purpose, was, I think, less conscious, and perhaps more profound. I would see it as being concerned with the establishment of **identity**, which I think is closely allied with a sense of shared purpose. My sense was that our client, through rapid growth, was suffering from a diminution in their collective sense of identity which had previously been derived from membership of a cohesive, successful group, small enough for mutual influence to contain the diversity of views and aspirations in a 'shared' sense of purpose.

Intuitively they understood that a sense of collective identity was a source of competitive advantage; it would give them a potential advantage over other consultancies with less cohesion around a shared sense of purpose. While we thought this aspiration, albeit not articulated in such a way, was entirely sensible, we had serious misgivings about how they wanted to achieve it – by launching, at a major London venue, their new set of values, inspired by which they imagined their employees going forth into the world all marching to the same tune!

We doubted whether it was even possible for a small group of people to articulate a set of values on behalf of a whole organisation, which would be likely to be so lofty and generic as to be more or less useless. Our experience of such attempts had been that they tended to generate more cynicism than inspiration.

However, as I explained earlier, we managed to persuade them that a thorough exploration of their currently **enacted** values, might enable them to get back in touch with what they thought was important about the firm they had created.

My reason for relaying this vignette is that I think it is a good example of a firm who sensed the need to re-establish a sense of **purpose,** although in this case, rather mistakenly in my view, through an attempt to articulate a collective sense of values.

A further example illustrates, rather clearly, the difficulty when there is a fairly clear statement of mission, but a significantly different sense of purpose held by two different groups of people in the organisation:

I was working with a United Kingdom charity whose mission was to 'save lives through improving early diagnosis, developing new treatments and preventing all types of breast cancer'. For one faction in the organisation this meant allocating the lion's share of funds into clinical research towards understanding and treating cancer, while another faction was more interested in educating women in life-style changes to **prevent** the onset of cancer, and ensuring and promoting access to early diagnosis and treatment.

Inevitably work in clinical research attracted different types of people to those attracted into education and promotion, and an uncomfortable schism developed over the years, about what was valued in the charity and how funds were allocated. I was brought in by the CEO because it became apparent to him that this difficult conversation could no longer be avoided. This required courage, but some difficult nettles were grasped and a change process emerged. I am not intending to narrate this here, but I do go into more detail about this kind of emergent and inductive change process in my final case study.

This short vignette illustrates the importance of rather rigorously addressing the two questions of mission (the what), and purpose (the why). In this case the mission was fairly clear, but one group of people joined the organisation because their purpose was to engage in clinical research, and their sense of **identity** was to a large extent derived from their association with clinical research.

The other group's purpose was to help women avoid or mitigate cancer, and they attributed much of their sense of identity to their role as educators. Both purposes appeared to be quite valid, but each required a different kind of operational model, and this charity did not have the funds to resource both.

IDEAS FOR ACTION

• Reflect on your own purpose: What difference do you want to make to your organisation? This is a question which, when I ask it, often floors leaders, who have not thought beyond implementing the objectives of the company. In my view this is not enough; a leader has responsibility for the qualitative life of the organisation, and some might see beyond that to the wider society and the environment.

• When you are about to embark on some major project or initiative, ask yourself, 'Is this congruent with my purpose?' If congruence is not immediately apparent, then ask yourself, 'What purpose is it serving?'. A sense of purpose is not immutable as your context changes, and maybe your purpose has shifted, or another purpose has emerged, and that is useful information; sometimes we find our sense of purpose by interrogating our actions, but I am suggesting you keep asking yourself the 'why' question, as you take up an 'attitude of inquiry'.

• Conduct some 'appreciative inquiry' among the people who work for you, asking the question, 'When are we at our best?'

Appreciative inquiry is a co-operative search for the best in people, their organisations, and the world around them. It was developed at Case Western University as an approach to change, as an antidote to the more conventional one which starts with a problem to be addressed. Case Western came to the view that this 'deficit' approach to change was counter productive. It is a methodology we used a lot at Ashridge, and is based on the following propositions:

   o In every society, organisation or group, something works well.

   o What we focus on becomes our reality, created in the moment.

   o The act of asking questions of an individual, organisation or group influences the group in some way.

o People have more confidence in creating the future relationship (the unknown) when they carry forward parts of the past (the known).

o If we carry parts of the past forward, they should be what is best about the past.

I came to incorporate this 'appreciative stance' into all my work with leaders and organisations and I commend it to you as a leader. It's quite simple really; you begin any kind of performance or project review with, 'let's start with what's working well', and expand from there; in this way you re-frame problems into constraints – what might be getting in the way of us doing more of what is working well. I say it's simple, but many of us have been inducted into our professional world as problem-solvers and it is actually quite a difficult habit to change.

When you too have learnt to take this stance, you will find that it generates a positive sense of purpose because people find purpose in what they do well.

LESSON 12: STRATEGY AS A DYNAMIC LEARNING PROCESS

For this lesson I am drawing on a chapter I wrote for a book entitled 'The New Strategic Landscape' (Verity, 2012). The concept of strategy influences, either implicitly or explicitly, much management thinking and practice, and it tends to be informed by a particular view of what an organisation is. How this view is understood and applied has important implications for how we make sense of our experience as leaders and facilitators of strategic change.

Most approaches are still informed by the prevailing orthodoxy which I discussed at some length in my first letter. I proposed a radical alternative, a perspective which sees organisations as 'Complex Social Processes' (Stacey et al., 2000), and is radical in the sense that it challenges most of the core assumptions inherent in the orthodox way of thinking about organisations. This has significant implications for the conceptualisation and practice of strategy.

CURRENT APPROACHES TO STRATEGY

The twin pillars of orthodox management thinking, efficient causality and scientific psychology, have formed the bedrock of most Western management teaching until this day, and still constitute the dominant managerial discourse – and this of course includes thinking about strategy.

The school of strategic thinking which has had most influence in business can be described as the school of 'strategic choice – a transformational process in which organisations adapt to environmental changes by restructuring themselves in an intentional, rational manner'. There have been a number of writers broadly within the school of 'strategic choice', and the one who is probably most familiar to managers is Michael Porter (Porter, 1980). He suggested that leaders had three main types of choice: 'Cost Leadership' strategy, a 'Differentiation' strategy or a 'Focus' strategy.

There is a generic methodology that is implied by the notion of 'strategic choice' which is quite familiar to most managers, consisting of some form of SWOT analysis, followed by identification of options, then choosing and implementing a strategy.

Most senior managers, and anyone who has been to business school with their emphasis on rational analysis, will recognise what is essentially a process of aligning the company to its environment. We are familiar with it and it appears to have some face validity, so we probably have not thought to question this established and habitual way of approaching business strategy.

However, if we closely examine some of the assumptions that inform the school of strategic choice, many of them appear to be at best, obsolete, and quite probably wrong.

The first assumption is that environmental changes are largely identifiable and that future states can, by and large, be predicted. We now realise that we live in a highly complex and unpredictable world, and this has almost become a truism. The idea that managers can predict future states and base plans upon them, does not resonate with our lived experience.

Furthermore, while one firm is working out its strategy, so are all its competitors, either formally or informally. As each player acts into its competitive landscape, so it is deformed, and as all competitors in a market are simultaneously acting into the 'market' landscape, it is clear that the combined impact is complex and dynamic. The 'market' of course, despite all the talk about its 'invisible hand', does not exist independently of the businesses and the consumers who create it. They are all participants in a process of interaction, affecting it and being affected by it at the same time. When you think about it, this seems common sense, but we have developed a habit of thought which speaks of 'the market' as a set of impersonal forces having an independent existence outside of the companies who compete with each other. From the perspective which I have been advocating and which informs this book, this way of thinking does not make much sense.

This realisation – that we are affecting and being affected by our environment at the same time – calls into question another assumption of the strategic choice school, the notion of linear causality, where one thing affects another in a clearly defined way. With this linear assumption unintended consequences are usually seen as the result of poor planning or poor implementation. As I suggested in letter one, unintended consequences are inevitable.

THE EMPEROR HAS NO CLOTHES

Increasingly, managers are finding that the conventional nostrums of management theory do not explain their lived experience of unpredictability, complexity and lack of control. On the whole they tend to assume that this is either because they are not applying them properly, or it is because they do not know all they are supposed to know – someone out there has a solution. However, when theory does not explain experience, the sensible thing to do is develop a better theory, and this is what 'complexity theory', or a version adapted to the social nature of organisations – which has informed many of the principles and lessons in this book – offers.

I now want to suggest the implications of this perspective for you as a leader when you come to addressing the 'how' question, usually known in business jargon as developing strategy.

IMPLICATIONS FOR STRATEGY

Acting with intention requires managers to formulate strategic intentions (anticipating **possible** outcomes) in the knowledge that they cannot predict outcomes.

This aphorism from Patricia Shaw (Shaw, 2002), that strategy is the interaction between chance and intention, is worth repeating, because it suggests that what you need to do, having formulated a strategic intention, is to work with, and learn from the outcomes that actually emerge, rather than spend precious time in analysing 'what went wrong'. This suggests two core strategic activities: formulating intentions, and responding to consequences.

A CASE STUDY

When working for Ashridge Consulting, a colleague and I were invited by a division of a reasonably large engineering group to help them with their 'strategy'.

Each 'business' within the group had its own infrastructure, in particular its own sales force, and quite understandably staff saw this site as the source of their livelihood, and the sales people strove to win orders for it, often in competition with other members of the same group.

An emerging set of powerful global customers now sought a more integrated response, expressed in the jargon of the day as a requirement to be a 'global player', a 'virtual company', particularly in the areas of price, quality and service. These customers were threatening to withdraw their business unless this supplier 'got its act together'.

THE PROCESS THAT EVOLVED

We were invited to attend a meeting of the 'change group', which was effectively the Board with one or two additional people. This group had identified a number of strategic issues which they thought needed addressing, and their plan was to nominate some staff to task groups, bring them all together at a conference and 'set them off' so to speak. They wanted us to design and manage this for them, and then 'train' the groups in how to lead strategic change, and get 'buy in'. We argued that their model of strategic change, whereby they identified the strategic issues and assigned people to tasks, would neither ensure that they were addressing the most important issues nor that anyone would 'buy in'.

Instead we persuaded them that a process whereby a large group of managers met over two days to identify the issues, and organise themselves around those issues would be more likely to create 'buy in', and stimulate the organisation's innovative capability. This idea was strongly resisted by some members of the Board who saw it as usurping their 'right' to decide what the issues were, and it challenged their assumption that their view would be the 'right' view. However, it seemed to resonate with the Chief Executive's experience of the limitations of the usual 'top down' approach to the formulation of strategic intention, and he agreed to what he saw as an innovative 'process' proposal.

We started with a two-day workshop for about fifty managers to begin a dialogue about what becoming 'global' would entail. We had three process intentions in mind; one was for the CEO to express his general intention without being too specific about the 'how; the second was to expand and deepen the quality of communicative interaction through creating opportunities for people to start talking and addressing problems in groupings that crossed their normal country, site or national boundaries; and the third was to mobilise the self-organising potential of the group to prioritise and take action.

The workshop was a new experience for most participants, and by their standards it was quite messy, but they also found it stimulating and exciting, many meeting their opposite numbers in other countries for the first time. On the first day we had some well-thought-through 'design', to introduce people to the 'global' intention, and identify the issues that this gave rise to. We asked Board members to participate in the group discussions, and from time to time to take up their role as the Board, and sit in the middle of the room, responding in real time to these issues as they came up. Some of the Board were very uncomfortable with this, but for most participants it symbolised something totally different and welcome in terms of management style, and the only question was whether it would be sustained.

On the second day we designed on the hoof in order to get to a manageable number of issues and to have some people taking ownership of these issues.

THE CHANGE INITIATIVE GROUPS

Five change initiatives formed, and we subsequently worked with each one to help them define what was really important in the broad area they had chosen, what could usefully be a 'project', and how to tackle what could **not** be turned into a project. The group concerned with customer service, for instance, started by defining four parameters of customer service. They then identified the processes which had the greatest impact on those parameters, what was needed to improve each of these processes, and ended up with an impossible list of projects! They then tried to prioritise the list, and finally came to realise that the final outcome of all this work would be to solve only a few problems, and not bring about any real change in what they began to see was a fairly deep-rooted attitudinal issue.

The question then became how to have a wider impact, how to **engage everyone** with the issue of customer service, so that everyone started to think of what they did in terms of its impact on the four parameters. The members of this group began to get themselves invited to operations group meetings, to explain their analysis, point out some of the problem areas in specific terms to specific groups. Some groups accepted the analysis and initiated their own activities to tackle the problems, and other groups were less willing to 'own' their problems, but such is organisational reality. Nevertheless, the members of the customer service group now saw themselves as leaders of a **change initiative** rather than members of a project team.

Some six months later we brought these groups together with the Board to review their activities, to learn together, and to develop further initiatives. This was the process designed to learn and respond to the emerging consequences of enacting the strategic intention.

COMMENTARY

This example highlights, in my view, the importance of maintaining both stability (providing a clear intention and a process structure), and creative instability in the process of working strategically. On the boundary between stability and instability, so the theory goes, lies the possibility of optimum creativity. In organisational terms this means working on the boundary between the formal and the informal, and this is one of the ideas which informed the overall design of our work.

We started with a reasonably large grouping, which we kept working in one large room (we did not have break-out rooms) in order for people to have a better sense of themselves in a wider context thereby stimulating connectivity. Within some broad parameters we invited them to explore **their** reality, to explore what the issues were, and to enable groups to form around the issues which emerged (self-organisation), rather than have senior management assign individuals to what they thought were the issues (management control).

Some senior managers were indeed not initially convinced that the 'right' issues had been identified, but we encouraged them to let this rather messy process of self-organisation unfold, rather than have them impose their own change agenda.

Finally, we realised how important it was that senior managers did in fact join the change groups but not as the group leader. They were thus not excluded from the process as they would have been in a 'bottom up approach', but were able to influence it by participating in the informal processes of the organisation, as opposed to exerting their influence through their formal leadership role, evoking compliant responses to the exercise of formal power, and inhibiting the organisation's potential for innovative self-organisation.

The consequences of this way of working were to provoke a different pattern of conversation, which provoked, excited, and disturbed in equal measure, and a set of strategic change initiatives emerged which were indeed owned by the whole of the senior management group.

IN CONCLUSION

The perspective I am proposing suggests that organisations continually emerge in an unpredictable way as they evolve into the unknown. Strategy, from this perspective, is merely the process whereby senior people orchestrate a conversation about future intentions and possibilities, based on their best anticipations of market opportunities, and a realistic assessment of the company's capabilities. It assumes that no group in the organisation has a monopoly of wisdom, that mobilising the collective intelligence within an organisation is more likely to come up with creative but sensible ideas, than an overly engineered, linear planning process, and that 'strategy', at its best, is an experimental and innovative process. There are, of course, exceptions to every rule, when single individuals or elites have for a while appeared to successfully drive a company's strategic development through the force of their personalities and particular creative vision. Our culture loves a hero and we are inclined to massage the evidence in favour of the hero myth, but it is always questionable how 'single-handed' such a process actually was. In the long run the evidence suggests that participative approaches to strategic development are more sustainable.

IDEAS FOR ACTION

Let me finish with some general ideas for action which flow from the lessons I have advocated in this book.

- It is helpful for you to think of yourself as being in charge but not in control. This requires you to act with intention (anticipating possible outcomes) in the knowledge that you cannot predict precise outcomes. What you need to do is to work with, and learn from the outcomes which actually emerge, rather than spend precious time in analysing 'what went wrong'.

- Relieve yourself of the expectation that you should always know what to do – you will only discover this through engaging in processes of conversation.

- It is more important and useful for you, as a manager/ leader to turn your attention to how things actually get

done (informal processes of conversation), and decide what
to do next, rather than designing over-engineered systems
and procedures in the belief that this is how things *ought* to
be done.

- Systems and procedures are merely codified and 'routi-
  nised' conversations – at best they will represent good
  practice, in for example quality maintenance, safety,
  recruitment etc. At worst they may become an obsolete and
  cumbersome set of procedures which inhibit innovation.
  See them for what they are, conventions made by people
  which can be changed by people.

- Inquire into what works well and encourage more of it.

- You need to engage in both the formal and the informal
  processes, paradoxically maintaining stability/consistency
  and provoking novelty and innovation at the same time.

- You need to minimise power differentials by encouraging
  a sense of *shared* responsibility, being clear that you do
  not have the monopoly of wisdom, but that by pooling our
  shared intelligence and experience and working *together,* we
  can solve any problem.

- Encourage people to speak their truth, and legitimise
  disagreement. The possibility of innovation emerges out of
  diversity and the interaction of difference.

- Change starts locally. It is far more effective to foster local
  initiatives and experiments than to embark on costly,
  formalised 'whole organisation' change programmes

In conclusion, I want to offer a brief summary of some of the main
themes about leadership which emerge from this book.

AN EMERGING VIEW OF 'QUALITY' LEADERSHIP

- The ability to operate in both the formal (managing
  today's business/getting results) and the informal (fostering
  initiative, challenging habits and assumptions, engaging

people in strategic conversation) organisation processes simultaneously.

- A 'systemic' perspective – the ability to see the organisation as a pattern of interconnected interactions (context), where a shift in one part may well have unexpected and unintended effects in another part.
- The ability to handle paradox (e.g. simultaneously maintaining stability in today's business, while provoking innovation).
- The ability to accept, understand and work with the normal politics of organisations.
- A capacity for reflection; a willingness to resist acting in order to be seen to be doing something, to please someone, or to demonstrate your status or prowess.
- An awareness of how you 'show up', and a willingness to risk becoming more of who you are, rather than who you think you are supposed to be.
- The ability to develop and work with your team as first among equals.
- A willingness to take the time to engage others in the process of decision-making where appropriate.
- The ability to clearly articulate a sense of purpose and strategy, and to foster participation in implementation.
- The maturity to engage and mobilise rather than assert control.
- The courage to act into uncertainty with intention, knowing that nothing turns out exactly as you expect, and to respond creatively to what emerges.

BILL CRITCHLEY
JANUARY 2021

REFERENCES

ARGYRIS, C. 1977. Double Loop Learning in Organisations. *Harvard Business Review* (September-October).

BATESON, G. 1972. *Steps to an Ecology of Mind.* New York: Ballantine, 1978.

BEISSER, A. R. 1970. *The Paradoxical Theory of Change.* In Fagan, J. and Shepard, L.L. (Eds) *Gestalt Therapy Now.* Palo Alto, CA: Science and Behavior Books.

BENNIS, W. G. 2003. *On Becoming a Leader.* Cambridge, MA: Perseus Publishing.

BINNEY, G., Williams, C. & WILKE, G. 2005. *Living Leadership.* Harlow: Pearson Education Ltd.

BOURKE, J. 2020. The Key to Inclusive Leadership. *Harvard Business Review* (March).

CAMILLUS, J. 2008. Strategy as a Wicked Problem. *Harvard Business Review* (May).

COLLINS, J. 1994. *Built to Last.* London: Random House.

COLLINS, J. 2001. *From Good to Great.* London: Random House.

CRITCHLEY, B. & CASEY, D. 1984. Second Thoughts on Team Building. *Management Education and Development,* Vol.15, Pt.2, pp163-175.

HEIDEGGER, M. *Being and Time.* Oxford: Blackwell, 1978.

HENDERSON, R. 2020. *Reimagining Capitalism in a World on Fire.* New York: PublicAffairs.

KAUFFMAN, S. A. 1996. *At Home in the Universe: the search for laws of self-organization and complexity.* London: Penguin.

KUHN, T. S. 1962. *The Structure of Scientific Revolutions.* Chicago; London: University of Chicago Press.

MASLOW, A. H. 1954. *Motivation and Personality.* New York: Harper & Brothers.

MEAD, G. H. 1967. *Mind, Self and Society from the Standpoint of a Social Behaviorist.* Chicago: Chicago University Press.

MORGAN, G. 1997. *Images of Organization.* Thousand Oaks, Ca; London: Sage Publications.

PORTER, M. E. 1980. *Competitive Strategy: Techniques for Analyzing Industries and Competitors*. New York: Free Press.

REVANS, R. W. 1965. *Science and the Manager*. London: TBS The Book Service Ltd.

RODENBURG, P. 2007. *Presence*. London: Michael Joseph.

ROVELLI, C. 2014. *Seven Brief Lessons of Physics*. London: Allen Lane.

SARTRE, J.-P. 1955. *No Exit and 3 Other Plays*. New York: Random House.

SCHEIN, E. H. 1992. *Organizational Culture and Leadership*. San Francisco: Jossey-Bass.

SHAW, P. 2002. *Changing Conversations in Organizations: a Complexity Approach to Change*. London; New York: Routledge.

STACEY, R. D., GRIFFIN, D. & SHAW, P. 2000. *Complexity and Management: Fad or Radical Challenge to Systems Thinking?* London: Routledge.

VERITY, J. 2012. *The New Strategic Landscape: Innovative Perspectives on Strategy*. Basingstoke: Palgrave Macmillan.

WATZLAWICK, P., WEAKLAND, J. & FISCH, R. 1974. *Change: Principles of Problem Formulation and Problem Resolution*. New York: W.W. Norton & Co.